MABEL
A LIFE
MERCER

ALSO BY JAMES HASKINS

Nat King Cole (with Kathleen Benson) (1984)
Bricktop (with Bricktop) (1983)
Lena Horne (with Kathleen Benson) (1983)
Katherine Dunham (1982)
I'm Gonna Make You Love Me: The Story of Diana Ross (1980)
James Van Derzee: The Picture Takin' Man (1979)
Scott Joplin: The Man Who Made Ragtime (with Kathleen Benson) (1978)
Voodoo & Hoodoo: Their Tradition and Craft (1978)
The Cotton Club (1977)
The Life and Death of Martin Luther King, Jr. (1977)
Diary of a Harlem Schoolteacher (1969)

MABEL

A LIFE

MERCER

BY

JAMES HASKINS

ATHENEUM

NEW YORK

1987

Atheneum
Macmillan Publishing Company
866 Third Avenue, New York, N.Y. 10022
Collier Macmillan Canada, Inc.

Library of Congress Cataloging-in-Publications Data

Haskins, James, 1941–
Mabel Mercer : a life / by James Haskins.
p. cm.
Discography: p.
Bibliography: p.
Includes Index.
ISBN 0-689-11595-4
1. Mercer, Mabel, 1900-1984.   2. Singers—United States-
-Biography.   I. Title.
ML420.M388H4 1987
784.5—dc19
[B]

Macmillan books are available at special discounts for bulk purchases for sales promotions, premiums, fund-raising, or educational use
For details, contact:
Special Sales Director
Macmillan Publishing Company
866 Third Avenue
New York, N.Y. 10022

10 9 8 7 6 5 4 3 2 1

Printed in the United States of America

To Peggy Benson

"It Was Worth It (That's What I'll Say)"

Contents

ILLUSTRATIONS

Lisa Rhana portrait, 1946 (Adde Wallin-Beach Collection)

With Joe Carstairs, Bart Howard, and friend, Nassau, Bahamas, late 1940s (Bart Howard Collection)

Mabel, 1950s (UPI/Bettman News Photos)

Lisa Rhana charcoal portrait, 1964 (Adde Wallin-Beach Collection)

Mabel with Harry Beard and Adelaide Wallin-Beach, 1965 (Adde Wallin-Beach Collection)

Lisa Rhana pastel portrait, 1968 (Adde Wallin-Beach Collection)

Mabel and Bobby Short (Adde Wallin-Beach Collection)

South Carolina, 1972 (Adde Wallin-Beach Collection)

Mabel's seventy-fifth birthday party, 1975 (Will Craik and Adde Wallin-Beach Collections)

Mabel receiving an honorary doctorate from Boston's Berklee College of Music, March 1975 a) with Harry Beard, William Craik, and Harry's sister, Pearl Lemert b) with Alec Wilder (Adde Wallin-Beach Collection)

Mabel at Cafe Lafitte in Philadelphia (Adde Wallin-Beach Collection)

Mabel and Jimmy Lyon at the London Playboy Club, July 1977 (Adde Wallin-Beach Collection)

Mabel at Cleo, fall 1977, (Will Craik Collection)

With her dogs and cats at her Red Rock farm (Will Craik Collection)

Washington, D.C., February 23, 1983, receiving the Medal of Freedom from President Reagan (Adde Wallin-Beach Collection)

Mabel, 1984 (Bart Howard Collection)

ACKNOWLEDGMENTS

THE FRIENDS AND FANS of Mabel Mercer who helped me with this book were not just willing, they were eager to do so. I've written a number of biographies, yet rarely have I been given such enthusiastic support. The people who talked about Mabel Mercer for this book not only applauded the idea of a biography of Mabel, but also seemed to welcome the opportunity to talk about her. Almost to a man or woman, they often spoke of her in the present tense, as if she were still with them, as indeed I suspect she is.

Whatever sense of Mabel Mercer, human being, is contained in this book is due to people who knew her and loved her: Will Craik, Adelaide Wallin-Beach, Bart Howard, Loonis McGlohon, and Joe Carstairs offered their time and hospitality and went out of their way to provide photographs and other memorabilia. Bob Adams, Allen Carter, Peter Conway, Eddie Jaffe, Rosetta LeNoire, Julius Monk, and Ronny Whyte shared their memories of Mabel and also suggested other sources of Mabel memories, as did Charlie Briggs, Beata Gray, Christine Lyon, Father Lee Smith, and Rex Reed.

Charles Kuralt put me in touch with Loonis McGlohon; David Litofsky and Judy Bell provided material on Mabel's recordings; Frances Brock Davies was helpful on dates; Nelson R. "Dick" Alford, Jr., and Arnold Caplin provided other important documentation.

Further research led to helpful responses from John Alger, Marlene Cameron, Mrs. Al Griener, Brian Hedley, Phyllis King Day, Andee Milstock, John A. Morton, Jr., Walter Richie, Lawrence Sharpe, Peter Spivak, and Sam V. K. Willson, each of whom supplied photographs, clippings, anecdotes, or advice. Arthur S. Koykka, director of Project Remember, "a national index of the gravesites of over 5,500 notable and newsworthy Americans," wrote to ask that I mention that project, so I will.

Patricia Allen-Browne traveled not only to the New York Public Library, main branch, the Lincoln Center Library for the Performing Arts, and the Schomburg Center for Research in Black Culture, for photos and other material from whose Bricktop and Mabel Mercer collections proved invaluable, but also to Chatham, New York, where Mabel lived for more than thirty years. Ann Kalkhoff found material at Brooklyn Public Library. Halimah Brooks provided assistance in Los Angeles. Kathy Benson helped to pull it all together.

INTRODUCTION

I FIRST MET MABEL MERCER, or rather was in the company of
Mabel Mercer, in the early part of 1976, in the living room of
an apartment on Fifth Avenue. It was late winter, I think, maybe
February. I had been invited to a cocktail party for some reason
by someone whose name I no longer recall; and of all the people
gathered there that evening I somehow only remember Mabel.
Thinking back now, I do recall that it was rather cold and wet
as I waited for the crosstown bus to come and that I was standing
in slush. I could see gum wrappers, Popsicle sticks, and other
remnants of the previous fall, things caught in the street before
the first snows of winter came.

In any case, I had of course heard of "Mabel," as her friends
called her, knew who she was, had heard that she no longer

had the voice she once had but that she was still "the same grand lady she always was."

I remember wanting to go to the party for little other reason than to be able at some later point in my own life to say that I had seen and heard Mabel either singing or speaking—such are the things that legends are made of. In my right mind and under ordinary circumstances I would not have gone out of my apartment that cold winter's evening for anything short of an emergency; nor do I even remember why I had gotten the party invitation in the first place. Perhaps the host thought that Mabel might be a good subject for a book, or an article. Mabel's friends were always thinking about her that way. But of course then I had no such idea in my own mind. At that time, I hadn't even thought of doing a book on Bricktop, whose autobiography I was to help write and who was a close friend of Mabel's. As a matter of fact, at that time I assumed that Bricktop was long dead and had no idea that she was very much alive and living about ten blocks from me on the West Side of Manhattan.

The apartment where the party—actually, it was more like an audience—was being held was understated in its elegance. There was no music playing, no loud chatter. Just a rather large living room with very good drinks and excellent food. Men and women, mostly middle-aged and older, well dressed and tanned, well heeled and confident, moved about casually acknowledging each other, stopping to chat for a moment, then proceeding on to a corner where it looked as if there were a receiving line. Not knowing anyone there except the host, I stood and surveyed the room, acknowledging those people who acknowledged me, pretending to belong. Before long I realized that what I thought seemed like a receiving line was indeed just that. People would come into the room, get a drink, chat with whomever they knew, and then move to that corner to meet Mabel. After a while it became clear to me that I was conspicuous because my movements had not been the same as everyone else's, which is to say I hadn't "greeted Mabel."

My host, who had noticed this by now, came over and asked me, "Have you greeted Mabel yet?" "No," I replied, and so I joined the line which, surprisingly, seemed to move quickly. When I finally reached "the chair," I found a lady resplendent in a royal-blue silk dress. She sat on the edge of the seat, with her bag beside her and a cup of tea on the table next to her. Alongside, a rather short, balding man stood greeting everyone, and both of them smiled as they met each guest.

I saw a look of puzzlement cross both their faces when I appeared next in line—mine was a face that neither of them knew. To his great credit and skill, my host bounded over at that moment to introduce me, and smiles and hellos having been exchanged, my audience was over. Such are the things that legends are made of!

But I'd had my audience, however brief; I could say I'd met Mabel Mercer. She was now part of "my legend." Now I, too, could refer to her as "Mabel."

I did not then start thinking about writing a book about her, nor even an article. That came later, when, talking with Bricktop, I got to "know" Mabel through her, and to share Bricktop's love and respect for her. I never got to know Mabel personally and, to paraphrase something Dave Garroway said in the 1950s, feel that I am "a little poor in life" because of that. But I have come to know her through the memories of those who were close to her, and share that knowledge here.

In the following pages, you will meet the Mabel I first met—the gracious lady—and discover as I did the "other" Mabel, whom only those closest to her knew. Hopefully, between the two, you will see the real Mabel—at least to the extent that she ever would allow—the little "Golliwog" from Wales whom the world came to know and love for her unique, storytelling way with a song, the virtual orphan who became the adopted mother of everyone who ever came under her spell.

James Haskins
Oxford, Maine
June 1987

MABEL

A LIFE

MERCER

I

MABEL'S
EARLY YEARS

SHE DID NOT SPEAK about her early years often. Her friends suggest that this was because her childhood may have been unhappy. According to actress Rosetta LeNoire, her friend for more than forty years, "No one ever told me this, and certainly Mabel never talked about it, but I wonder if there wasn't something that no one will ever know. Something that hurt her when she was very young." Or, it may have been that she simply did not like to talk about the past. Will Craik, Mabel's friend of more than thirty years, says, "I don't think she deliberately tried to conceal anything about her past. What's done is done. She wasn't interested. She was interested in the here and now. We would talk and talk and talk, and sometimes we'd sit and not talk about anything, but she rarely talked about her younger days. She'd say, 'Oh, that's water over the dam,' or, 'That's spilt milk.' " The real reason is no doubt a combination of both, for Mabel was a private person with a keen sense of what was appropriate and what was not, and she had grown up with an awareness that the circumstances of her birth were not "appropriate," in Staffordshire, England, at the turn of the century. For one thing, she was born into a family of show people. For another, her father was a black American musician.

Mabel later described her mother's family as "bohemian," full of painters and people in show business: Three uncles and her maternal grandfather were painters, and according to Mabel legend not just painters but artists with works in the Royal Academy. Her maternal grandmother, an aunt, and her mother were singers and dancers. While London and the Continent were the ultimate of success, there were small halls everywhere in the British Isles where talented performers could make a living of sorts, bringing respite to careworn workmen and shopgirls, spreading the late-nineteenth-century jingoism stimulated by the looming Boer War in South Africa. One of the popular songs in the halls went:

> We don't want to fight,
> But, by Jingo, if we do,
> We've got the ships, we've got the men,
> And we've got the money, too.[1]

Minstrelsy was popular at the time. Imported from the United States, its presence in Britain represented something like a third incarnation—originating among black American slaves on Southern plantations, it had been taken up by white entertainers, who performed in blackface, then transported abroad where it was performed by non-American white entertainers in blackface. Formularized and replete with ugly caricatures of blacks by the late 1800s, its popularity had diminished greatly in the United States, but it was still strong in England. Even in England, however, the appearance of troupes of real blacks, often billed as "real Africans" or "real Coons," was something special, as it had been since before the middle of the century.

Ira Aldridge, the black American tragedian, had toured the English provinces doing Shakespearean plays with the British actor Edmund Kean, although on Kean's death in 1833 Aldridge decided that racism in the British theater was more than he cared to deal with and left Britain for the Continent, where he enjoyed a distinguished career for more than thirty years. On the other hand, William Henry Lane, known on the stage as "Juba" and billed as "The Greatest Dancer in the World," came to London with Pell's Ethiopian Serenaders in 1848, married an English girl, and remained in London until his early death, well before the age of thirty, in 1852.

That same year, Harriet Beecher Stowe's *Uncle Tom's Cabin* was published, and plays based on the story were soon among the offerings of every repertory company on both sides of the Atlantic. There were active Anti-Slavery Societies in Britain, France, and elsewhere that welcomed performances of such plays, not to mention personal appearances by such former slaves and Abolitionist spokesmen as Frederick Douglass, who were celebrated and feted and otherwise made much of.

In the late 1890s, what one writer called "the lament of the lost" was popular in London. John Lawson was a hit throughout the British Isles with his short drama *Humanity*, and the "colored artists" Brown, Newland, and LeClerq also did quite well with *Black Justice*, a dramatic piece similar to *Humanity*.[2] That is not to say that the audience's sympathy ran deeper than a good cry at the theater: although there were romantic liaisons between British women and black Americans, these were not in any way celebrated. Such a liaison between the English-Welsh singer who used the stage name Mabel LaBlanche and a black American musician whose last name was Mercer was not one to be spoken of, either by LaBlanche's family or, much later, by the little girl named Mabel who resulted from that relationship.

All that is known about Mabel Mercer's father is that he was a black American musician. The public story is that he died before she was born; the private one is that Mabel was conceived without any foresight at all on the part of her parents-to-be.

Says Will Craik, "The kindest way I ever heard it put was, 'Her father's name was not on the birth certificate.' Somebody told me that. But other people have told me they thought that's how she got the name Mercer." It is not even known for sure whether her father ever knew of her existence.

No such mystery attended the result of that coupling in Mabel's mother's mind. On February 3, 1900, in Burton-on-Trent, Staffordshire, she bore into the world a girl baby and no doubt was relieved that the child had light skin (described in later years as "like cream with a little coffee in it") and blue eyes. The only real hint of her black parentage lay in her dark, kinky hair. Mabel LaBlanche went back on the road shortly afterward, touring Australia, New Zealand, and South Africa and leaving little Mabel in the care of her grandmother. The British music halls were flourishing, and a woman who was accustomed to the roar of the crowd and the smell of the greasepaint, not to mention a weekly salary, was not about to leave all that to raise a child. As one writer described these women, "They marry, bring children into the world, but still hanker after the 'halls,' the applause of the crowd, You can't wonder at it; domestic life rarely appeals to the old 'pros.' "[3]

As a child, Mabel had little contact with her mother, who was generally on the road somewhere. Adelaide Wallin-Beach, Mabel's friend during her last thirty years, recalls, "Every once in a while, I'd say, 'That's what my mother said to me as a child,' and she'd say, 'That's what my *grandmother* said when I was a child.' Little by little, she'd come out with the story: her mother was in show business; she did not see her often; she lived with her grandmother; her grandmother had also been in show business."

"My mother's family—my grandparents' family . . . it was a madhouse," Mabel once said. "They were all artists—thank God, because I didn't have to grow up with any stuffy—you know—but singers, musicians, painters."[4] Retired by that time, Mabel's grandmother maintained the home base of the eccentric and creative family, and some of Mabel's fondest early childhood memories were of the Liverpool kitchen redolent with the smell of baking bread (ten loaves every Monday), the fragrance of the Sunday "joint" of lamb, the aroma of the traditional Parkin cake, a loaf of oatmeal and treacle (hard when baked and soft a week later), on Guy Fawkes Day, and of mince pies. The feel of the moist steam from the kettle on the hob, the tinkle of teacups, the smell of toasting bread on a long-handled fork over the hot coals of the huge stove, were sensations that forever after meant comfort and security to Mabel.

Because she did not see Mabel Senior often, in little Mabel's mind everything about her mother was special. She was very beautiful and she could sing and she could dance. She loved plants and flowers and had a sense of communion with them that Mabel seemed to recognize even then. "When I was little, my mother would never take a walk without a pair of garden shears," Mabel told jazz critic Whitney Balliett in 1982. "She'd snip things from our garden and she'd snip things hanging over our garden wall or any garden wall. She considered such strays legitimate picking, and she'd put them in water to root, and plant them. So I went out one morning and dug up some of our neighbor's flowers and brought them back in my apron, pleased as Punch that I had them roots and all. My grandmother was leaning out the window watching me, and she came right out and took down my panties and spanked me—and my goodness, the embarrassment! My face was as red as the flowers I'd taken."[5]

But that didn't stop Mabel from loving flowers and plants, for her mother did, and her mother was special. Mabel suggests that she also got her fine diction from her mother. Somewhat later, when Mabel was ten or twelve and developing enough of a singing voice to interest her mother: ". . . she'd take me into an empty theatre where she was working, and she'd go up to the top gallery and make me stand down on the stage and sing. I was a very shy child, even with her, but she'd say, 'All right, sing! And I want to understand every word!' "[6]

At some point, Mabel acquired a stepfather, but he was as

little known to her as her mother was. They were usually on the road. Mabel remembered that her mother was short and her stepfather was tall and skinny and that their vaudeville act was called Ling and Long. One part of the act, which she saw occasionally as a child, was exciting and unforgettable. They would dress up in white tennis clothes and step out on a simulated court, and the lights would go down and they would toss luminous clubs back and forth across the net. "My stepfather had invented the luminous clubs," Mabel told Whitney Balliett in 1972, "and you'd see these squashy balls of light drifting back and forth through the dark, and it was a beautiful spectacle."[7] Ling and Long were a comparatively successful act in British vaudeville, which was heavy on acrobats and jugglers, and so Mabel saw even less of her mother once her mother remarried.

When Mabel was seven, she began to see even less of her beloved grandmother and of the bohemian aunts and uncles who made her early childhood exciting, if still lonely. When she reached school age, she was sent away to board at a Catholic convent school in Manchester and henceforth saw her family only during summers and school vacations. The convent school was called Blakely, and nuns became family for young Mabel. They instilled in her a strong Catholic faith that would never falter in all her years and that would inculcate in her a sense of the otherworldly, a sense of the universe as God's creation and of every living thing as God's child, that would inform her decisions and her opinions for the rest of her life.

She was left-handed as a child, a condition, called "gammy-handed," that was thought to be a serious problem and correctable with the right amount of discipline. Apparently Mabel obeyed, although it must have been difficult for her to change the hand with which she painted, a pastime that delighted her as far back as she could remember. In a way, the Catholic Church helped her to correct her gammy-handedness. "For a long time, I didn't know my left from my right," she told Whitney Balliett in 1982, "and the way I'd tell would be to make the sign of the cross, which you always do with your right hand. That would show me which was my right—and which was my right foot, so that I could start a dance step correctly."[8]

It was at Blakely that young Mabel first began to realize that she was different. Her gammy-handedness was the least of it. She also discovered that her family's profession was highly unacceptable in polite circles—"Vaudeville was on a very low rung of social affairs. Anyone who was on the stage was looked upon as . . . oh dear, awful people."[9] For the rest of her life, she took conscious steps not to appear "bohemian."

Finally there was the matter of her uncommon heritage. Her family had never sat her down and explained to her the circumstances of her birth or her parentage, although apparently they had prepared the nuns, who were ready with answers when she had questions. At first, Mabel kept her questions to herself, if they were even yet formed in her young mind. Her earliest inkling that she was different was that her hair was not like that of the other girls.

The girls nicknamed her "Golliwog," a term that she could not have found in any dictionaries of the time. It derived from a series of children's books illustrated by Florence Upton in 1895 which portrayed a grotesque black doll and which had inspired the manufacture of little black dolls with black woolen hair. When Mabel asked the nuns what "Golliwog" meant, she was told, in simple terms a child could understand, the circumstances of her birth and parentage.

She was half-black, the nuns explained to her. Her father had been an American Negro. She had African blood, although her freckled face and blue eyes and cream-colored skin belied that. The telltale mark was that kinky hair. "Golliwog," the nuns apparently told her, meant that she had African blood in her. Whether, at base, it meant "nigger" or "mixture" in Mabel's mind depends on how she chose to tell the story, and perhaps also on the perceptions of friends and interviewers to whom she told it over the years. Nearly everyone recalls that she told it lightheartedly, as a comic story. According to Will Craik, "She always spoke like that was one of the happier periods of her life." She named her house up in New York's Columbia County after the convent, Blakely. One of her dogs was also named Blakely. But on some occasions she invested the story with sadness and hurt. In 1975, she was interviewed by William Livingstone, editor of *Stereo Review*: "At school all the kids thought I was rather odd. They'd never seen anything like me. I was the only one, you see. They christened me Golliwog, which was an affectionate term, because the 'golliwogs' the children had were little black dolls, with black woolen hair. The one who sat next to me in the refectory at the convent— Queenie Vail—had long flaxen hair down to here. I never had any more than I've got now, and it was the bane of my existence. . . . I remember one little girl said to me, 'Oh, *you*'ll never get married.' And I said, 'Why?' 'Your hair's too frizzy,' she answered. 'No man will ever marry you.' And another kid said, 'We'll turn you upside down and sweep the floor with you.' And I got terribly upset because I had golliwog hair."[10]

Mabel was wont to "accentuate the positive," and given her situation—Mabel was always a survivor—it is likely that she decided that the best course was not to take offense at the nickname and not to emphasize any more than she could help it her newfound black blood. There were no such things as pomade or curling irons at Blakely, nor were these items available back home, so Mabel had few avenues of experiment when she determined to make her hair tossable over her shoulders like the other girls'. Given the paucity of possibilities, she settled on a very clever solution: she tied strings—or ribbons when they were available—to her curls, and having achieved at last a free-flowing mop, practiced tossing her ribbon tresses, taking her hand and sweeping them back, so that she could achieve what she seems to have regarded as the epitome of little-girldom. No doubt, the other girls teased her about this, but not in an especially hurtful way. It was just another delightful side of the strange, shy little girl who some of the older ones suggested might be an African princess. After a time, she came to be regarded as a sort of mascot at the convent school, rather like one of the ugly but beloved golliwog dolls.

Still, Mabel became an exceptionally self-conscious child. "I don't know how I ever became an entertainer," she told Livingstone. "It was absolute agony at school when I was called on to recite a poem or something. I would turn scarlet, my knees would knock, and my lips would tremble so that I could hardly pronounce the words. And there I was, the child of performers, and I couldn't get over it. Horrible, horrible."[11] More than likely it was Mabel's self-consciousness and tendency to mumble that caused her mother, on one of her rare visits to home and Mabel, to decide that she needed some practice with her diction and ability to project her voice.

Such rare attentions from her mother did not have much effect on the formation of Mabel's character. One thing no doubt became clear to her as she grew up: the nuns—and by extension the Catholic Church—were the purveyors of the gospel of the life of little Mabel Mercer. They told her the truth and loved her still, which was more comforting than the artistic and less stable environment provided by her family, who, it appears, steadfastly refused to discuss the circumstances of her birth with her. Recalls Peter Conway, who met her in the late 1940s and later became her friend, "When she asked who was her father, she was told that she should never ask that question. It became quite clear to her that she was illegitimate."

Mabel spent her summers with her grandmother in North Wales, times that were luscious in her memory, filled with flowers and trees and streams, with hills and valleys and small cottages, with stray dogs and cats and flocks of birds and all the other opulence of God's living universe. "I remember endless fields of poppies and wheat and blue cornflowers and how we'd return from long walks decked out with bracelets and necklaces of daisies and buttercups, and I knew that one day I had to have a place in the country," she told Whitney Balliett in 1972.[12] Hopefully, her mother and stepfather were sometimes able to join her there, or at least some of the assorted aunts and uncles whose pursuit of the arts mandated an occasional return to nature. Mabel drew and painted and took long walks and probably was far too shy to pose embarrassing questions, like Who am I? Based on her later attitudes and behavior, one suspects that she realized that things like nonmarital interracial liaisons, and the fact of the issue thereof, were simply not talked about. And trying to be a good girl, and trying to be loved and accepted, she did not ask questions. She was an obedient child, and so when she was around twelve and suggested to her grandmother that she would like to be an engineer, on being informed that this was not suitable for young ladies, she dropped the idea.

She had realized by this time that she did have to come up with some ideas of what to be, for at age twelve she only had two more years at school before she would be cast upon the larger world and forced to make her place in it. In Britain, one completed basic schooling at that age, and then went on to further schooling or work or marriage, depending on one's circumstances. Given Mabel's station in life, there was no question but that she would have to go to work. Apparently, Mabel was not leaning toward nunhood and spending the rest of her life in the cloistered and comfortable milieu of the convent school. Perhaps that was because she realized she was a Golliwog and would never really fit in. Or perhaps her relatives suggested that there was more to life than what she had found at Blakely Convent.

Mabel was to make much of that life, and to educate herself much more fully through reading and travel, but Blakely Convent and her family had provided her with a firm base on which to build. As her friend Will Craik put it, "It always amazed me: she left school at fourteen and started working, but she spoke the most beautiful English—grammatically correct, excellent diction—and she could talk about an enormous number of subjects. I always wondered where she got such an education. At fourteen, kids over here would be considered middle school dropouts. I suppose it's the old adage about travel being broadening."

Mabel may well have dreamed of completing her schooling at Blakely and then joining her mother and stepfather on the road, for if there was a strong sense of unfinished business in her, it would have been to get to know her peripatetic mother. But in 1912, when Mabel was as old as that century, her mother and stepfather undertook an extended tour of North and South America, and when World War I broke out they were stranded there, unable to return. "Wars seem to have directed my life," Mabel told Whitney Balliett in 1982."[13] Mabel did complete her schooling in 1914, but when she went into show business she joined not her mother's and stepfather's but her aunt's vaudeville act.

The aunt was Rhoda King, later famous as featured player in *Chu Chin Chow*, who at the time was using the stage name Mademoiselle Du Roche and traveling in a family singing and dancing act with her husband and two children. The children had been born in the proverbial stage trunk, and welcomed Mabel into the act and into the household, although, as writer Roland Wild reported in 1953, they could not resist teasing her about her hair and playfully pushing her head under a water tap to see if they could wash the light brown from her skin.[14]

With the addition of Mabel, the act was billed "The Romany Five," the gypsy implication added to explain the presence of Mabel.[15] It was still a family singing and dancing act, and most of its members did both. Mabel's small, sweet soprano voice was apparently not deemed adequate to the stages of British music halls, and she was assigned the role of dancer. Two cousins who were also in the act taught her the rudiments of step dancing, similar to tap dancing. She had grown to her full five feet of height by then, although her swan neck and erect convent posture made her seem taller. The freckles that dotted her nose and emphasized her high cheekbones, and her shy blue eyes, gave her a fresh-faced appearance. The baneful "wooly head" made her seem rather exotic, and apparently did not affect the group's business.

They went all over England, playing week-long engagements in the various towns on the British vaudeville circuit and traveling from one town to the next on Sundays. Mabel remembered that they would hire their own railroad coach and put a placard in the window announcing who they were. As the train chugged through the countryside, farmers and shopkeepers, housewives and children waved, and when they stopped at a town depot the local citizens cheered, sometimes because the troupe had played in the town before and been well received. Mabel loved going from town to town, for in the small world of vaudeville everyone knew one another. She remembered the excitement of seeing old friends and the suspense of finding out where they would appear on the bill. Placement in the entertainment lineup was crucial, and the major indication of popularity and salary. In Mabel's recollection, her family's troupe never made it to the coveted position of closing act, but they did make it to next-to-last act a couple of times. The bad memories she did not care to mention, but the life of a second-rate vaudeville team was also fraught with coldhearted managers and drafty houses and the constantly looming fear of being stranded a hundred miles from home.

By the time Mabel went on the road, the golden days of British vaudeville were drawing to a close. The introduction of the first American "super films" in London—D. W. Griffith's *Birth of a Nation (1916),* and *Way Down East* (1920), among them—would soon change the way the public viewed entertainment. By that time, too, salaries for music hall stars had increased to the extent that music hall operators were forced to raise admission prices. People who had been accustomed to paying a shilling or two for a four- to five-hour show would soon object to paying more.[16] Still, plenty of first-class acts were still doing well, among them the comedian J. W. Rickaby, a native of Lancashire, with his signature song "Silk-Hat Tony" or "They Built Piccadilly for Me." Then there was Gertie Gitana, with her silver top hat and songs like "Silver Bell." Animal acts were still extremely popular, as were acts that were heavy on physical prowess—the American boxer Jack Johnson offered a music hall act in London in 1914 while waiting for British producer C. B. Cochran to line up a fight. Finally, Cochran arranged a match at the Velodrome D'Hiver in Paris against another American, Frank Moran, on June 27, 1914. The following day, the Archduke Francis Ferdinand was assassinated in the Bosnian town of Sarajevo.[17]

If the war, which stranded her mother and stepfather in America, was a source of despair for young Mabel Mercer, it also provided her opportunity. Britons were never more eager for respite from the cares of war, and the Romany Five worked steadily. Unfortunately, the two cousins who had taught her to step-dance were male, and eventually they were called to the service of their country. The act broke up, and Mabel was forced to go out on her own. It was not a course that she would voluntarily have chosen at that time, but there was little else that she could do. Marshaling every bit of courage she had, and telling herself that she could sing and dance well enough to get by, she joined a troupe of girl dancers. She was about sixteen at the time. (While according to most published sources, Mabel did not go out on her own until after the war, Loonis Mc-Glohon, her good friend and one of her last accompanists, is quite sure that she spoke of being on her own when she was sixteen.)

The group was small-time and local, and when it reached Manchester, Mabel auditioned for a job with the Tiller Girls, a group rather like the Rockettes whose home base was Manchester but which sent out smaller troupes to the provinces. Her career with the Tiller Girls was short-lived, however, lasting only until, as Mabel put it, "the head man saw me": "He said, 'Oh, out with *her*, she's not right in the line.' I was so different, you see, with my wooly head."[18]

According to one story, the next time she applied for a job with a dancing troupe, she attempted to alter at least the color of her hair by soaking it in a henna dye. Something went wrong and when she appeared for the audition her head looked as if it were caked in red plaster.[19] Eventually she joined another troupe whose director was not so choosy, and managed to support herself by picking up whatever jobs she could find.

Later, she joined a colored show called *Spades and Diamonds*, an "American Negro minstrel show," or the best the American producer could manage with the talent he had available. Mabel got to sing in that show—inevitable songs like "That Coal-Black Mammy of Mine." She didn't pay much attention to the lyrics, or if she did, she kept her sense of their irony to herself. She was far more interested in earning a regular salary than in questioning what she had to sing to earn it. She was also intrigued by the other members of the troupe. "Now *that* was a first experience," Mabel told William Livingstone. "I had never known any colored people, never *met* any. Isn't that funny? My family never discussed anything, and I was the only one at school, so I just took it for granted that I was one of a kind. And finding these others was like a dream. I was delighted. We were all different shades but all the same."[20]

Settling in a boardinghouse in the black section of a London suburb, she came to know the Boucher family, whose matriarch soon informed Mabel that it was not appropriate for a young girl to be alone. Mabel needed little convincing to move in with the Bouchers, whose daughters, Ena and Madeleine ("Dicky"), she came to regard as sisters and with whom she would remain close for the rest of her life. The Boucher family was black, and with them Mabel had the opportunity to experience a warm and nourishing black family and to bring out into the open the part of her that she had been forced to suppress as a child.

Mabel joined another black show, which was called *Colored Society*, and stayed with it for at least two years. It was a review, with very good singing and dancing as well as comedians, all of whom were either Britons of mixed blood or Africans and on whose strengths the director attempted to capitalize, although the result was rather strange. Loonis McGlohon, who served as Mabel's accompanist during the last years of her life, recalls her saying that she "didn't think the producer had ever seen a real minstrel show, so it was a very curious mixture. She said, for example, that the costumes were a mixture of Polynesian and American Indian and African—grass skirts and flowers and so forth. The opening scene was a dance. There were six blacks, and she was the youngest. I'm not sure how many of them had come from Africa, but several of them were very well-trained opera singers who had studied in Italy. She said the first scene was like a jungle set, with vines hanging around the stage and tom-toms in the orchestra, which played an African beat. They all came on and did a very primitive dance that was half African and half Indian, with a lot of 'Oooo, ooo' with the lips. Then she said there was a bell tone on the piano, at which point they stopped, stood in a straight line, and began to sing in Italian the sextet from *Lucia*. [Mabel sang the soprano part.] And she said that there was a gasp—an audible gasp— from the audience, and the singers were very perplexed. To them it was perfectly natural to break into Italian opera, because they'd all been trained in it. They felt there was nothing unusual about this until one night when they came out of the stage door and were following some people who had been in the theater. Mabel heard the people say, 'Isn't it marvelous how this director has trained these savages to phonetically sing Italian.' So, she realized, for the first time, that these trained singers were not being taken seriously." And she realized, yet again, that by virtue of the part of her that was black, she would always be different.

She remained with the show throughout the war, through the Zeppelin raids and the nighttime blackouts that made it necessary to hold hands as she and her friends negotiated the lightless streets on their way home, and through the influenza epidemic that produced the first Mabel Mercer male impersonation.

"This was in 1918, I think," says McGlohon. "That was the year of the flu epidemic—I remember her tying it in with the year of the big flu epidemic, and it seems to me that it was 1918. They were on the road, playing cities like Birmingham and Chester, breaking the show in to go to London. I think she said that in the smaller cities they just used piano, and in the bigger cities they added two or three guys. Anyway, the conductor, who was also the pianist, fell sick with the flu and had to go to the hospital. Mabel knew how to play the piano, and the director said, 'Mabel, you'll have to play piano,' and so she did. She became the rehearsal accompanist, or the show accompanist, on the road. [She would still leave the pit to rush up onstage for her part in *Lucia*.]

"They got to London (the conductor had recuperated), and I think it was the final rehearsal before opening night when he had a relapse of flu and was sent back to the hospital. The director said, 'You'll have to conduct the orchestra, Mabel.' Well, it was unheard-of for a woman to conduct an orchestra—they now had a ten- to twelve-man orchestra for the London opening. She said, 'They'll never stand for a woman conductor.' He said, 'Well, I think we can solve that.' He took her to a tailor and had a tuxedo made for her. She said he tied a corset or something around her breasts to make her flat, cut her hair, and took oil and greased it down. She said by now she was sort of enjoying this charade and so she bought a monocle—just for kicks, she said. And then the director said, 'You can't talk, Mabel. I'm telling the orchestra that you're a very eccentric, temperamental African conductor—volatile. If they ask you anything, just sort of grunt.'

"She said that she got through the opening night, the second night, the third night. After the third performance, on the fourth morning, they were having breakfast. The guys knew who she was. When Mabel said, 'You know, I think it's a miracle that I've passed so far,' one of the guys said, 'No you haven't, Mabel, not exactly. Last night, after the show, my girl friend said, "You know, I've seen a lot of conductors, but that's the first Chinese fag I've ever seen." '

"It's not the kind of story that Mabel told very often. She was so ladylike and didn't like profanity or anything risqué. I was surprised that she told the story, really. But you know, she had that lovely gold-colored skin and very high cheekbones and could look Oriental under certain circumstances."

Bart Howard, who met Mabel in 1938 and was her accompanist from 1946 to 1950, remembers another story she told about her stint as an eccentric African conductor: "She kept getting mash notes from this guy. So eventually she made a date with him, and he met her at the stage door, and she was in a dress! And he said, 'Oh, my God,' and flew!"

That was undoubtedly the source of Mabel's later occasional appearances as a male impersonator. She had a great time as the eccentric African conductor. "Entertainers used to have what we called cigarette cards, their photographs with their names on them," she later recalled, "and when we got to Bristol I had my picture taken in my white tie and tails—and with a monocle, if you please—and someone put a cigarette in my hand. That was me as a conductor. And I had 'Musical Director' on my card."[21] Once in a while, she would don a tuxedo and monocle and attempt to sing in deep, throaty tones.

But by the time she was in her teens, the popularity of male impersonators was on the wane. They had been in great demand for some forty years before the war. In the 1870s there was Bessie Bonehill, who toured America in the early 1890s and while there received an average of a dozen marriage proposals a week. She died tragically young at the age of thirty-six, in 1896.[22] Then there was Vesta Tilly, "The London Idol," who specialized in the impersonation of male stars like the old-time Piccadilly Johnny, and who introduced a number of popular songs, among them "Following in Daddy's Footsteps."[23] Hetty King and Ella Shields ("Burlington Bertie, who rose at ten-thirty") capitalized on Tilley's popularity, and enjoyed quite a bit themselves. After the war broke out, however, male impersonators seemed somehow inappropriate.[24] Yet after the war, in the jazzy twenties in Paris, male impersonation enjoyed a resurgence in popularity, and Mabel Mercer would take jobs as a male impersonator if no other jobs were available.

When the war ended, Mabel teamed up with another girl in a dancing act, billed as Kay and Mercer. They dressed alike and attempted to look alike: although Mabel, who was only five feet tall, was actually taller than Kay and could do nothing about that, she did buy a curly wig so that her hairdo approximated Kay's. They worked in hotels and cabarets, and when they couldn't get by with just dancing, they tried singing and whatever else might please an audience. "My friend would do impersonations of Mistinguett [the French chanteuse], and we'd sing duets. I'd do a ballad alone—an Irving Berlin song or an American rhythm song. We'd tap-dance, and I even tried acrobatics, but I was as acrobatic as an elephant."[25]

During the war, travel between Britain and the Continent had been severely restricted. Once the war was over, British entertainers were free to travel in Europe, and Mabel and her girl friend did so. There was nothing, apparently, to keep her in England, for it seems that her mother and stepfather did not return, but remained in the United States once the war was over. Mabel had occasion to think often of her mother around that time, for in order to go abroad she had to get a passport, and in order to do that she had to know the answers to some very personal questions, like who her father was. When she approached her aunt with the problem, Rhoda King realized that the family could no longer dismiss Mabel's questions. However, that didn't mean the family had to answer them. "Go to Somerset House, Vital Statistics Division, and find your birth certificate," Mabel's aunt told her. "Then forget everything you read there."[26] Mabel did, but she didn't forget. She became keenly interested in her father, and from then on whenever she met a group of black American musicians she would ask them, "Did you know my father?"

Mabel and her girl friend took their act to Ostend, Belgium, where they performed at the casino, a huge place with three floors and lots of entertainers who toured the tables after their acts and collected tips to augment their small salaries. Mabel didn't like that custom, but the professional hostesses were friendly and called her over to their tables, where the men they were with were generous in order to impress the hostesses. There at the casino Mabel saw her first American band, and it was a *black* American band, to boot. "I thought oh, *this* is the *ultimate*," Mabel recalled. "If I could just perform like that! In those days

I was just trying to do a few shuffles and sing ballads. But I danced for them, and they engaged me. They must have thought I was the *funniest* thing they ever saw, because they were Americans, and I was still doing it all in my English way. But they were nice fellows, and I was *young*, and we had good times.[27]

If the war had brought trouble and pain to Europe, there was one good thing that came out of the experience: Europe met, and fell in love with, American jazz. Until that time, European musical supremacy had been unchallenged, and in retrospect, that was something else Europe lost in the war. But Europeans were too busy dancing to the new American music to think about it.

Europe, of course, was no stranger to American music—Europeans had heard "minstrel songs" and "plantation melodies," had experienced the cakewalk and a significant ragtime craze. But the new music called "jazz" was something else entirely, and when it was introduced by such a consummate musician as James Reese Europe, there was no way it could be ignored.

Europe had already become famous as the leader of a well-known black dance orchestra in New York when the United States entered the war in 1917. When Europe enlisted in the city's black regiment, its colonel, William Haywood, decided to take advantage of his talent. Haywood solicited $10,000 from a local businessman, Daniel C. Reid, a donation earmarked specifically to pay the best musical talent Europe could find to create a military band *non pareil*. The band, nicknamed The Hellfighters, arrived in France in February 1918, prepared not only to be the best marching band ever assembled, but also to break down into several dance orchestras or theater bands. They were an immediate sensation in France, and soon inspired other regiment bands to emulate their success—Lieutenant Tim Brym's and Lieutenant Will Vodery's were among the most notable. The word "jazz" became part of the European vocabulary—the French preferred the term *le jazz hot*—and came to symbolize the brazen cocksureness of the Americans who had come to liberate Europe. When the war ended, it symbolized newness, difference, a fresh beginning.

Even before the war ended, the management of the Casino de Paris had charged its black American drum soloist, Louis Mitchell, with going to New York to recruit a band. He returned with a seven-piece orchestra, which he called the Jazz Kings. Noble Sissle, drum major with Europe's band, was certain that after the war he and his friend and partner Eubie Blake could also find a red-carpet welcome in the City of Light. As he wrote to Blake on October 14, 1918, "Jim [Europe] and I have Paris by the balls in a bigger way than anyone you know."[28] Not a few black American soldiers, who were also musicians, never bothered to return to the United States after the war, and among those who did, there were many who jumped at the chance to return to the Continent. Early in 1920, Elliot Carpenter, a piano player in New York, was asked to find a group of musicians for a new club in Paris. Carpenter, who had not been to Paris himself, was skeptical of his ability to interest others in the venture. He recalled, "Two of the boys, Opal Cooper and Sammy Richardson, had just come back from the war. So I went to them and said, 'Do you guys want to go to France?' and they said, 'My God, yes!' "[29] They didn't even ask about money.

There was no question in the European mind that "jazz" equaled "black," and blacks suddenly found themselves in great demand as exotic creatures whose every movement exuded *le jazz hot.* Mabel Mercer was hardly the exotic black type—even then she was the ultimate lady—but she was all that was available, for while male black American musicians were not uncommon in Europe by then, there were few if any black American women.

Mabel did not join the band she'd met in Ostend permanently, although she would maintain contact with them and work with them from time to time. In the main, she continued to travel with her friend in their Kay and Mabel act, to Antwerp and Luxembourg and Brussels. In Brussels, Mabel learned to eat little pieces of fried garlic, cooked quickly in a pan. "I loved it so much that my boss had to tell me to stop—that I was ruining the act."[30] In Amsterdam, according to Mabel's friend the artist Beata Gray, someone pulled off her wig. Mabel "used to laugh merrily when she told about it." Only nineteen years old, cosseted as a child by both family and nuns, Mabel was beginning to spread her wings. But she was not carefree, and probably had not been carefree since early childhood. She had been through too much sadness. Says Rosetta LeNoire, "I think Mabel was born old."

The two-girl team was quite successful in getting work. Mabel, as would always be her habit, gave most of the credit to her partner, Kay, a Cockney girl whose imitations of Mistinguett had the French rolling on the floor. But one suspects that the shy Mabel found her own fans among European audiences. Certainly, both her singing and her dancing appealed enough to assorted acts to get her hired alone, which apparently presented no problem for her partner. The team had a tacit agreement that when one got an opportunity to work solo, she should take it, and when they were both free they would get back together.

London continued to be their home base, and it was there that Mabel, alone, joined another black American act, the John Payne and Roseman trio, which specialized in Negro spirituals. The group had lost its tenor, and Mabel was the replacement.[31] "We sang everything, a cappella and with piano accompaniment —lieder, Negro spirituals, French songs, 'Yes, We Have No Bananas,' 'Carolina in the Morning,' " Mabel once recalled. "One of the men had been a choirmaster, and it was he who caused me to start studying singing." She studied with the idea of becoming a mezzo-soprano and a concert singer. "I paid for my lessons by working in shows and singing in nightclubs," she told Whitney Balliett in 1972, "and that's no way to become a classical singer."[32] Nonetheless, the first time Mabel saw Paris was when she went there with the trio in 1920. Unfortunately, Paris was also where the act broke up after three years,[33] and although Mabel was able to get some work in Paris, it was not enough to keep her in a city with which she had felt an immediate affinity.

In the early Twenties, she worked with "The Southern Trio," starring Lord and Cabot, which toured the Continent. She also continued to work with her girl friend, and Kay and Mercer traveled with any number of shows. They worked with a circus and sang between the acts. They worked in a variety review that also featured the comedy dancing act Williams and Taylor. Mabel had a romantic relationship with Williams. Coincidentally, the Williams and Taylor act was similar in ways to that of her mother and stepfather, for one was tall and one was short, although Williams and Taylor had taken their inspiration from a popular black American comedy team, Flournoy Miller and Aubrey Lyles. Later, she and her partner were in a show called *The Chocolate Kiddies* (she wore a bouffant blond wig in that one) whose orchestra was, in 1925, an American group led by Sam Wooding. This show played Vienna as well as Yugoslavia and Constantinople, Cairo and Alexandria, and while it didn't do a lot for Mabel's concert singing career, it did much for her education. "I'd go out to the Pyramids every day," she told Whitney Balliett in 1972. "It was when they were excavating the Sphinx, and I remember the workers passing pails of sand along and singing chants, like the American gandy dancers."[34]

While in this romantic land, Mabel had another romance, or at least found herself an object of passion for "a gentleman from Turkey," as her friend Will Craik puts it. "I understand from Mabel that he was quite wealthy, and quite smitten with her," says Craik. "He was going back to Ankara to tell his family that he was going to marry her. She was still in Egypt when she got a letter from this gentleman, but it seems he had crossed up his letters: seems he had other women he was proposing to, and the letter intended for Mabel someone else got and the letter that Mabel got was definitely intended for someone else. She used to tell me, 'That's why you don't have to come to see me in Ankara these days.' "

Those were golden years for Mabel. "I wasn't making much money, but I was seeing the world, and if I'd become a typist or something I'd have been stuck in an office."[35] And during those years she traveled to enough places and met enough people to get, at last, an affirmative answer to the question, "Did you know my father?" According to the story, it was a man in Paris who said, "Yes, I knew him. He's playing in a band in the South of France." Also according to the story, Mabel went to see her father, but never identified herself. She only wanted to see him, and to finally put that one large question to rest.[36]

CHAPTER

II

PARIS, AND BRICKTOP'S

"PARIS WAS VERY EXCITING in those days," Mabel Mercer often said in her characteristic understated manner. Paris was Guy Fawkes Day, Christmas, and Mardi Gras all rolled into one, a perpetual Fourteenth of July. Everyone wanted to forget the war, to celebrate light and life, and the city swarmed with merrymakers, dancing in the streets, carousing in the clubs, and spending money as if it were about to be declared illegal. As F. Scott Fitzgerald recalled, there was so much money around that even when you were broke you didn't worry about it. If you had talent and charm, someone would take care of you. Paris was the mecca for writers, painters and sculptors, philosophers and philanderers, for the European nobility and rich Americans such as the cash register Cranes and the Singer sewing machine family—whose dollars went even farther than usual in France's inflationary economy. From the Left Bank cafés of Montparnasse to the tiny clubs on the narrow, twisting streets of Montmartre, where in 1920 the Commune Libre de Montmartre was founded for the purpose of indulging in revelries and parodies of political life,[1] expatriates from all over the world came to revel in all that had been taboo—cocaine and Bolshevism, Dada and Surrealism, and interracial, interclass, intragender, intramural sex.

F. Scott Fitzgerald called this wild decade the Jazz Age, and if there was anything for which the Paris taste was insatiable, it was jazz. So many black American bands and individual musicians were being imported that a substantial colony eventually arose in Montmartre. They hung out in Louis Mitchell's café when they weren't working, and spent their money as fast as they made it, much of it, according to Elliot Carpenter, "on those whores they had up there."[2] In fairness to the black American musicians, there were very few black women, American or otherwise, around. Florence Jones, wife of Palmer Jones, who had been the pianist with the band that had hired Mabel at Ostend, Belgium, was one of the few, along with Mabel.

Mabel loved being in Paris and kept returning to the city between engagements with touring shows. She, too, enjoyed the music and the all-night night life, but she loved the daytime Paris as well, when a different but equally energetic breed took over the streets—the bicycle-propelled delivery wagons, the pushcarts of the itinerant vendors, knife grinders, umbrella menders, the bustling shoppers hurrying from the butcher shop, where only beef and lamb were sold, to the pork store, which handled sausage, to the dairies, where chicken was sold along with cheese and milk, to the open-air flower markets. In Paris, Mabel found an entire city of fellow flower lovers, who would stop one another on the sidewalk and openly and loudly admire a single rose. Mabel liked to visit the flower market when she left work. "Dawn in Paris . . . nobody thought there was anything odd about visiting the flower market and having breakfast at dawn."[3] She took an apartment at the top of the Rue Pigalle and for the first time in her adult life had a home she could call her own.

In Paris, Mabel also found a very Catholic city, and dozens of venerable cathedrals from which to choose when she attended daily Mass, although the nearest was also one of the most impressive. The Sacre-Coeur, atop the Butte de Montmartre, was visible for many miles around Paris.

There were only two distasteful aspects to Paris, in Mabel's eyes. One was the official consciousness of race, which she had not expected to find and which she discovered when she applied for a cabaret license: "There was a place [on a form] where she was supposed to fill in her race," recalls her friend Adelaide Wallin-Beach, "and she had never been asked to do that before, and she didn't know what to put there. She went up to the clerk and asked, 'What can I fill in here?' and he said, 'Black, of course.' She told me she looked at him and said, '*Half* of me is white. I'm *just* as white as I am black.' He said, 'You're black.' "

Wallin-Beach remembers Mabel telling her about another, more striking incident in Paris, much later, after Wallis Simpson had become the Duchess of Windsor. "The Duchess of Windsor invited her up to her hotel, and Mabel started up the front way and was told she had to go by the back way. The Duchess was furious with the concierge." Mabel said she had never come up against such barriers in all the other countries she had been— not in England or Spain or anywhere else." Such incidents were rare, and since both insults came at the hands of the *petit bourgeois*, Mabel dismissed them.

The other disadvantage of life in Paris was the legions of open-air taxis, manned by the rudest daredevils she had ever encountered. Even the quintessentially well-mannered Mabel would, on occasion, give one of them his comeuppance.

She had not forgotten her upbringing, and although she enjoyed the wildness of Paris she did not get swallowed up by it. She loved the night life, the carefreeness. She enjoyed meeting the artists and writers who frequented the Montparnasse clubs where she worked—Ernest Hemingway and Gertrude Stein (she'd never seen a woman with a mannish haircut before), and Vincent Youmans, and F. Scott Fitzgerald—but she was not awed by them because they were all young together, and struggling together.

Mabel, perhaps, was struggling more than most, for she was never asked to be singer in residence at any of the clubs; she was simply a fill-in. The hot-blooded jazz style just wasn't hers. When Palmer Jones's wife, Florence, left Le Grand Duc, a tiny boîte on the Rue Pigalle, to open Chez Florence down the street, Mabel took her place, but while she made friends with both Gene Bullard, the manager (and the first black American pilot to win the French Legion of Honor), and a young black American busboy named Langston Hughes, she wasn't bringing in the customers. Bullard sent to the United States for a black woman who could give Florence Jones some competition, and that's how "Bricktop" (Ada Smith) got to Paris. Mabel was singing at Le Grand Duc when Bricktop arrived to take over in May of 1924.[4]

Bricktop was too busy trying to adjust to Paris and the tiniest club she had ever seen to pay much attention to Mabel, but in the small black colony of Montmartre no one was a stranger for long. "She was a striking girl," Bricktop later recalled, "but she didn't get a lot of work."[5] It wasn't long before Bricktop was wondering if she would soon be like Mabel, for no one had told her that the summer was dead in Paris—that everyone went to Monte Carlo and Cannes and Biarritz.

Unfortunately, the fall and winter were not much better. Bricktop remembered, "That winter we used to sit in Le Grand Duc hour after hour and not a soul would come in, except maybe Herbert Jacoby, who was a literary man in those days, along with the French writer Louis Aragon, and maybe one of the French composers of Les Six. They would sit there and look at me for hours. Jacoby later became one of the biggest cabaret impresarios."[6] Mabel, meanwhile, had gone over to Chez Florence.

In the fall of 1925, seventeen-year-old Josephine Baker arrived to star in *La Revue Nègre* and by virtue of her "banana dance" (clad in nothing but a girdle of bananas) created a sensation. By the following year, American and French impresarios had begun to milk the market for jazz spectacles, and the rush of copycat revues was on. Mabel was able to get some work in these from time to time, for although most of the performers came from America, there were always spots for a local girl to pick up.

Meanwhile, there was room for more refined black revues, like Lew Leslie's *Blackbirds of 1926*, starring Florence Mills, which opened first in London and then toured the Continent. Mabel got a job with *Blackbirds*, in the chorus, and played in both London and Paris. She also understudied Mills in a show called *Silver Rose*.[7] Like Mills, she had a sweet soprano voice, and Mabel might have been able to carve out a niche understudying Mills and singing songs that Mills made popular. In 1927, however, Florence Mills was stricken by appendicitis and died, tragically, in her early thirties.

Also in 1927, Paul Robeson arrived in London with *Showboat*, the Jerome Kern and Oscar Hammerstein II adaptation of Edna Ferber's novel. Mabel auditioned at the Theatre Royal in Drury Lane and won a minor part.[8] She was impressed by the thirty-year-old Robeson, and when the city of London feted him and his wife, Essie, as if they were visiting royalty, she was proud of the part of her that was black. She grew to love *Show Boat* and dreamed of one day singing the part of Julie, but she seemed destined always to be a member of the chorus, or a stopgap singer. While Mabel, by virtue of being at least half black and of having considerable experience in show business, especially as a dancer, benefited to some extent from the Negro vogue in Paris in the 1920s, she never got a chance at stardom. Like Florence Mills, she was a bit too refined for the European idea of what a black woman should be—they liked them hot and sassy, like Josephine Baker. Mabel was not about to engage in inappropriate behavior, and she couldn't sing jazz, even if she had wanted to. She was still taking voice lessons, but she was no longer seriously dreaming of being a concert singer. She continued to perform male impersonations on occasion, but she hardly considered making a career of it. According to Bricktop, "Around town there was the feeling that Mabel wasn't going anywhere. No one sold Mabel's talent short—it was just that they felt she didn't have the personal aggressiveness to put it over."[9]

Bricktop, by contrast, was a feisty little woman with more than enough personal aggressiveness to make it in the jungle world of show business, although she had no compunction about admitting that it was Cole Porter who really made the difference for her. He came in one evening in the fall or early winter of 1925, and as it happened Bricktop was singing one of his songs. But he wasn't interested in her singing. She recalled, "What he wanted to know was, could I dance? I couldn't believe it when he asked, 'Can you dance the Charleston?' "[10] Cole Porter told Bricktop that she had "talking feet and legs," and he wanted her to entertain at his Charleston parties.

Through Porter's Charleston parties, Bricktop began to meet "the top hosts and hostesses of Paris. This was the time when there were big, big parties." Elsie de Wolfe, then Lady Mendl, Elsa Maxwell, Dolly O'Brien, Arturo Lopez, the Rothschilds, Consuelo Vanderbilt, and all their friends liked the way Bricktop entertained at private parties, and they began showing up at Le Grand Duc at night. Soon, the marquee outside the club was changed to read BRICK TOP, and eventually she took over the club entirely. Bricktop was a "saloonkeeper par excellence," as she put it, a consummate hostess who made her patrons feel as if they were in their own living rooms. She had "the best people," from the "royalty" of the United States— the Porters, Michael Farmer and Gloria Swanson, the Dolly Sisters—to the true royalty of Europe—the Duke of Windsor, Lord and Lady Mountbatten, and assorted other kings and counts. There were so many of them, in fact, that by 1931, casting aside all doubts of the effects of inflation and the crash of the New York Stock Market, Bricktop decided to open a bigger club in the space that had once been occupied by another club called the Monico.

"It was at 66 Rue Pigalle—a great big room that could seat about a hundred people, with a couple of smaller rooms, a bar and a kitchen. I had Hoyningen-Huené do the lighting—he did the lighting for a lot of theaters, but he was most famous as a society photographer. Neil Martin did the decorating. The walls were lined with banquettes, and Hoyningen-Huené lit them from behind and created a cozy, kind of mysterious atmosphere. There were heavy patent-leather curtains across the door, and as you approached you could see only shadows—the silhouettes of people's heads. The carpet was red, the banquettes were red and black, everything was done in red and black—and with that lighting, well, when it opened in November 1931, it was the talk of Paris."[11]

It was also a major responsibility. Famous for her ability to keep one eye on the door and the other on the cash register, Bricktop knew that even she could not handle alone the management of the new club. She had recently married Peter Ducongé, a musician from the United States, but he was not interested in helping her run the club. "I had to find someone else," said Bricktop, "and my first and only choice was Mabel Mercer."[12]

When she told others that she wanted to hire Mabel, their first reaction was, "Bricky, who wants to hear a soprano at twelve o'clock at night?" But Bricktop wasn't interested in Mabel for her singing. "I wanted her because she was very well-met—very shy and reserved, a lady. Beautifully friendly, but never familiar. I knew I could sit her down at a table and know that she wouldn't use any bad language or tell any dirty jokes, and that she'd laugh at the right times. She also drank nothing but champagne. Mabel was someone I knew I could trust—and an entertainer besides. It was a decision I made as a business-woman."[13]

For her part, Mabel knew all about Bricktop, and Bricktop's. In the still comparatively small Negro entertainers' colony in Paris, everyone knew everyone else. Mabel had attended Bricktop's wedding to Peter Ducongé, and knew most of Bricktop's clientele. According to Bricktop, Mabel's first reaction was, "Oh, great, Bricky, I'd love to." But then she did decide she ought to discuss the matter with Harvey White, whom she was dating at the time.

White was a black American musician who had been highly successful in New York and now was playing in the band at Chez Florence, where Mabel was currently singing. Mabel may have wanted to discuss the matter of salary with him, for she had no head for business and undoubtedly would not have been so quick to answer Bricktop in the affirmative had it not been explained to her that her position stopped short of handling the club's business matters. She liked the charming-hostess part of the job description, and the idea of a steady job in Paris appealed to her. It may have been Harvey White, however, who persuaded her to ask for a comparatively large salary for her services.

". . . When she came back a couple of nights later," Bricktop recalled, "and I asked her how much she wanted, she said two hundred francs. That was big money, good money. She really couldn't have gotten it anywhere else, but as a businesswoman I was willing to pay her that much because I knew how much help she would be to me. As it turned out, I was a big help to her, too. Mabel is the first to say it, and has said it many times: 'I became a star at Bricktop's.' "[14]

And so, the almost legendary partnership began between the ultra-lady mulatto from Staffordshire and the "one hundred percent American Negro with a trigger Irish temper" from "Alderson, West-by-God Virginia." Mabel was thirty-one, Bricktop was thirty-seven. Both were getting heavier than they had been in their younger days, both had freckles, both had skin like cream with a touch of coffee, both wore their frizzy hair pomaded and slicked back. Mabel was shy and unaggressive, Bricktop was open and forthright. Mabel was social, Bricktop was sociable. Mabel hated everything to do with business, Bricktop knew how many bottles of champagne were consumed in the space of an hour. Cole Porter used to say, "If you want to talk social, talk to Mabel; if you want to talk money, talk to Brick."[15] They were a good team.

Mabel had no trouble at all handling the charming-hostess part of her job. Few among the star-studded clientele of Bricktop's were strangers to her, for they had heard her sing at other Paris boîtes. The ones she did not know were easily charmed, among them Harry K. Thaw, who had still not lived down the notoriety of having shot and killed the architect Stanford White a quarter of a century earlier. When it came to meeting her other responsibility—that of singing—however, Mabel was not so accommodating. It wasn't that she did not want to sing for the patrons, it was just that the room was so large and the hundred-odd voices so loud . . .

Recalled Bricktop, "Night after night I would arrive to hear the bandleader complain, 'Mabel hasn't sung yet.' When I told her that she simply had to get on the floor and sing, Mabel's answer was always the same: 'Do you think they really want to hear me?'

" 'I don't know about them,' I'd say, 'But *I* want to hear you.'

"The clients really didn't take to her voice. After she'd sung, I'd go over to the tables and say, 'Well, what did you think?' and the clients would say, 'Wellllll, Bricky . . .' And I'd say, 'But she's an awfully nice girl.'

"She was, and they found that out, and pretty soon when the clients came to the club, they'd say, 'Tell Mabel hello' or 'Tell Mabel to come and have a drink.' "[16]

Bricktop, the businesswoman, was determined to get her two hundred francs' worth and make an entertainer out of Mabel. When she had to agree with Mabel that Mabel's voice just wasn't up to the acoustics of the crowded room, she suggested that Mabel go to the individual tables and sing. People could request certain songs, and Mabel would go right to their tables and sing them. But, of course, the other people complained that they couldn't hear her. So, she began to use a megaphone. "I used a megaphone long before Rudy Vallee," Mabel later said. "I'd go from table to table, sit and sing the song the people there wanted, but with a megaphone for the rest of the room."[17]

Bricktop still wasn't satisfied. "Stop waving your hands around," she'd say. "Cup them in your lap, like a lady." Mabel listened, and followed the advice. Meanwhile, she was adjusting on her own to the circumstances in which she had to perform —finding what worked and what didn't, for her and for the clients.

"That sort of intimate singing is tricky, you know," she told Whitney Balliett in 1972. "You can't *look* at the people you are singing to. They get embarrassed. So you look at the ceiling or the far corner of the room, and then they can stare at you and know that you won't look down and catch them. Sometimes we'd sing all night. . . ."[18]

Unable to look at those to whom she was singing because it would embarrass them, unable to use her hands in elaborately expressive gestures as she had on the stage because Bricktop told her not to, and unable to project her voice across the room without a megaphone because her voice simply wasn't strong enough, Mabel Mercer began to pay close attention to the lyrics of the songs she sang and the manner in which she sang those lyrics. By this time she had realized—"my critical decision and great disappointment"—that she was never going to be a classical concert singer.[19] But at Bricktop's she was making the first regular salary she had ever enjoyed. The patrons of the club still didn't think much of her voice when she tried to make herself heard at midnight, yet as the months wore on she could see that they were beginning to respond to her "intimate singing," to her sitting at their tables and singing *to* them, not *at* them.

She realized that they especially liked it when she sang about things to which they could relate—universal, human things like love and sadness. She invested the lyrics with as much meaning as was intrinsic to them. She began to look for songs whose

33

lyrics were, in themselves, poetry, or which told a story. She also began to emphasize the ironies in lyrics, to take a half-mocking approach, to sound ultrasophisticated and supremely wise and worldly, rather like the patrons of Bricktop's to whom she sang.

According to one story, Mabel also got a brief foretaste of the type of singing that would later become her hallmark. One damp Paris winter she caught a cold and actually stayed away from Bricktop's one night. Afraid to stay out two nights in a row, she went to work the next, although when she sang her voice was low and husky. To her astonishment, the customers loved it, and Mabel realized she could reduce the register of her voice without sacrificing its clarity.[20] Still, once the cold went away, the mezzo-soprano came back.

Cole Porter, who had a reserved table at Bricktop's whether he was even in Paris or not, provided a number of songs for Mabel to sing, "Love for Sale" among them. The song had a rather curious history. The idea came to Porter when he was at Zelli's on the Rue Fontaine, which employed gigolos and taxi dancers. When Porter asked one of the girls what she did, she answered, "I've got love for sale," and that struck Porter as a great title for a song. He wrote it and included it in the show *The New Yorkers*, which premiered in New York in early December 1930. In the original version of the show, Kathryn Crawford, playing a "lily of the gutters," sang it, accompanied in the chorus by June Shafer, Ida Pearson, and Stella Friend. But critics, among them Charles Darnton of the New York *Evening World*, objected to it as being in "the worst possible taste." In the show, the setting was changed to the Cotton Club, the famous Harlem nightclub, and the singer to a "colored girl." Still, even though Libby Holman and Fred Waring and the Three Girl Friends recorded the song, and many nightclub singers liked it, the song was banned on the radio.[21]

Mabel liked it. There was sadness in the song, especially in the lines: "Let the poets pipe of love/In their childish way,/ I know ev'ry type of love/Better far than they./If you want the thrill of love,/I've been thru the mill of love,/Old love, new love,/Ev'ry love but true love."[22]

Another Cole Porter creation became Mabel's theme song. "Just One of Those Things" was written originally for the 1935 show *Jubilee*, starring June Knight and Charles Walters. Mabel was also thirty-five that year, and the song appealed to her. She was still singing it forty years later. "Well, I've had my experiences, and I happen to know what I'm talking about," she explained to William Livingstone of *Stereo Review* in 1975. "I've always been on the sentimental side, but not maudlin. When you're young you cry a lot. I thought I'd never survive certain things in my life, that if it didn't go the way I wanted it to, life was not worth living. Later you learn to shrug your shoulders, and say well, it was great fun. 'Just One of Those Things' is not a sad song; it's very cynical, and I like to get a laugh on the line about a trip to the moon where nothing happens. We've all been in that situation, and some people in the audience respond to it with a laugh, others can't."[23] Cole Porter, who was notorious for *not* liking the way most singers rendered his songs, considered Mabel's rendition of "Just One of Those Things" the finest he ever heard.

She sang many other songs because the clients requested them—and because they asked for them, she respected those songs and invested them with as much meaning as she could. Jimmy Donahue, cousin to Woolworth heiress Barbara Hutton, loved Bricktop's, and he loved Mabel's singing so much that he found it best to ease away from it when he left Paris, and ease into it when he came back. According to Bricktop, "When he came to Paris, he would be at Bricktop's every night, and when it came time to return to the United States, he couldn't go cold turkey—so he'd call from the ship every single night. The band would play and Mabel would sing, and Jimmy would go to bed happy. The same thing would happen when he left New York to come to Paris: the telephone would ring and it would be a shipboard call from Jimmy wanting to hear Mabel sing 'My Belle' [from *Show Boat*]. And there'd be a call every night after that until he showed up at the club in the flesh."[24]

Then there were the songs that little-known people wrote for Mabel: if she could respond to the lyrics, and believed the clients could also respond to them, she sang them. One such song was "Thank You for the Flowers," written for her by "a young society lad," as she put it. "It wasn't terribly good, but it seemed to take everybody's fancy, and it was requested a lot. Porter and his gang of friends got tired of it, and decided they'd have me arrested if I sang it one more time. Sure enough, someone asked for it, and while I was singing it, a gendarme tapped me on the shoulder and led me off the floor. It was just a joke they'd cooked up between them."[25]

By the time that happened, Mabel was secure enough at Bricktop's to be able to take the joke. She also had the courage to request that anyone who lit up a cigar while she was singing be asked to put it out, and that became a rule at Bricktop's.

There were other rules: no woman was admitted without a gentleman escort, and everyone had to be properly dressed. Bricktop rarely had to enforce such rules, for her patrons were of high society and always appropriately attired. "There was an elegance and a beauty about it all that doesn't exist anymore," Mabel told Whitney Balliett in 1982. "People left their gold-and-diamond cigarette cases on their tables when they danced, knowing very well that they would be there when they returned. It was a champagne world."[26]

And it was a carefree one. Apparently, no one around had anything better to do than to dance and give parties and make music. When Bricktop's closed around five or six o'clock in the morning, everyone trouped over to the Breakfast Club or the Music Box. Mabel recalled the morning when "Louis Armstrong with his trumpet and Django Reinhardt with his guitar were playing for each other. I went home and to bed. I got up around noon and came down for some milk or something, and they were *still* there playing duets. People were so carefree in those days."[27]

Within a year or so, Bricktop and Mabel had settled into a comfortable business and personal relationship. They respected one another, and each deferred to the other in areas where either had greater knowledge or a greater emotional investment. Mabel, for example, made a point of being fluent in French, while Bricktop realized that she got greater mileage out of "fractured French," which her patrons found warmly comical. That is not to say that Bricktop did not behave correctly around royalty; she simply was not as emotionally involved with them as the Britisher Mabel was.

Bricktop: "I never had any problem feeling comfortable around the royalty that came to the club. . . . Mabel Mercer had an entirely different attitude. . . . Every time the Prince [of Wales] came . . . he just stunned her. When he entered the club, she stood at attention as strict as a member of the Royal Guard. There was no relaxing Mabel. The Prince represented *her* royalty. She was interested but never swayed by other members of the nobility who filled the place night after night."[28]

Mabel: "When you went to a party you never knew who would be there, and we were constantly being invited to parties. Brick was very strict about that: you can go to a party, but you don't sing; if you go to a party and sing, you get paid for it."[29]

Bricktop: ". . . one time in Paris, the night before Easter Sunday, Ramon Novarro was in the club. I heard him say, 'I can't drink after twelve o'clock.' I started to say, 'Why not?' But Mabel said, 'Shhh, Brick, be quiet. He's going to communion.' I said, 'What's that?' and Mabel said, 'Brick, don't be so ignorant.' . . . Mabel was a great Catholic, and she was right—I *was* ignorant. She'd take me into a church with her, and I'd say something like, 'Mabel, keep your hands off those statues or they'll put you in jail.' "[30]

Mabel: "We'd stop people as they were leaving and say, 'What's your favorite song? You won't be back for a year. Stay five minutes longer and let me sing your song.' "[31]

"The set," as the patrons of Bricktop's called themselves,

came in the spring and in the fall. "Every year it would be like meeting old friends," Mabel recalled—"the Indian princes, the Maharanee of Cooch Behar, and this one and that one. I knew them all and they were all *very*, very nice."[32] In the summer, the set went elsewhere, and by 1932 Mabel and Bricktop were following them. There wasn't much point in remaining in Paris, especially in August, when the entire city closed up shop and one had to locate new butchers and bakers. It made some sense for Bricktop's to relocate to the resort areas during the summer months, although it did not make economic sense to try to follow the set from one resort area to another as they enjoyed their respective "seasons." Moving Bricktop's meant moving everything from cooks and waiters to dishes and glassware, not to mention musicians and singers. They could not very well go to Deauville or Cannes or Nice for several weeks, and then move on to Biarritz. Bricktop chose Biarritz, whose season was only about five or six weeks long, because the set, which was pretty much scattered throughout the Côte d'Azur in the early part of the summer, tended to converge on Biarritz at the end. Located just above the northern border of Spain, on the Bay of Biscay, Biarritz had achieved its cachet when Edward VII, grandfather of the Prince of Wales, began to spend his summers there.

That summer of 1932, Bricktop took over the Merry Sol, right on the Mediterranean, for the month, and she and Mabel entertained, among others, the British nobility, who naturally carried on the family tradition. The Prince of Wales came opening night, and every night thereafter. At the time, he was the constant companion of Lady Thelma Furness, and that relationship caused no end of tongue wagging. Prince George, younger brother of the Prince of Wales, was also in residence at Biarritz that season. Known as a playboy, he was living up to his reputation that summer, but with Bricktop and Mabel he enjoyed being himself. Bricktop remembered, "[one] time a stray dog followed Mabel and me to the club. We were soaking wet—Mabel, me, and the dog—from one of those sudden Biarritz showers. The Prince and Edith Baker [American pianist, about whom the Prince was serious enough, apparently, for the Queen Mother to order him back to England in the middle of the Biarritz season] were there. We all sat on the floor, dried out the dog, played with her, and drank champagne."[33]

Beth Leary, a wealthy woman from New York and a close friend of Lady Thelma Furness, gave parties of thirty or forty people many nights at the Biarritz Bricktop's, and both Brick and Mabel were invited to entertain, individually or together, at any number of private parties. That first summer in Biarritz was so successful that they decided to return the following summer.

They were eager to open Bricktop's again that October, and it proved to be a banner season. Duke Ellington and his orchestra arrived in Paris in the spring of 1933, and Bricktop invited the entire entourage to be guests of the club. Even Josephine Baker went to Bricktop's that night (according to Bricktop, Baker's husband, Pepito, kept her away because he was afraid of Bricktop's influence on her), and when Mabel sang, no one was more attentive to her singing than Josephine. By now, Mabel was getting a reputation for being a genius with a lyric, and Josephine was fascinated with her delivery—her intimate way of first speaking the lyrics, then smoothly melting her speaking into singing. Josephine Baker would later incorporate many aspects of Mabel's style into her own singing.

As the summer of 1933 approached, Bricktop and Mabel prepared to take Bricktop's to Biarritz again, and inquired about taking over the Merry Sol for a second season. They were dismayed to learn that Jimmy Mussolini, who had been head-waiter at Bricktop's, had decided to go out on his own and had already secured a commitment from the owner of the Merry Sol. Bricktop had to settle for a space that was not nearly as convenient, or as posh.

As it turned out, however, no location in Biarritz was particularly lucrative that summer. The effects of the Depression had finally begun to take their toll on the wealthy Americans, as well as on the Europeans of wealth and nobility. Within a couple of weeks, Jimmy Mussolini and Bricktop had come to the conclusion that the only way to save the season for both of them was to join forces. Bricktop and Mabel agreed to become entertainers at Jimmy's, for he had the better location.

Still, the club was half empty most nights. Even the rich Europeans didn't feel like partying as much, and the wealthy Americans were practically nonexistent. In retrospect, Bricktop realized that she should have paid more attention to the financial news from abroad and tried to forecast how it would affect her business. Mabel, never having been one for business in the first place, was even more nonplussed than Bricktop. She was also more broke.

French inflation had been taking its toll on Mabel's comparatively substantial salary since she had first gone to work for Bricktop. In fact, from 1929 on, meat had been steadily higher in price and tougher in texture, milk had been paler, eggs smaller and dirtier. Even the flower market bouquets, without which Mabel could not live, had steadily increased in price and decreased in freshness. She had learned to be satisfied with a single bloom, and to be willing to forgo meat at a meal in order to have a flower to grace her table. In company with ordinary French people, she could not understand why, on the one hand, the French government was piling up a tremendous deficit, while on the other, it was lending huge amounts of money to Poland, Rumania, Germany, Hungary, and monarchist Spain. What both she and Bricktop did understand was that, given the dismal Biarritz season, they faced returning to Paris without enough money to live on until Bricktop's on the Rue Pigalle reopened.

Because there were still a few private parties to entertain at, they stayed on in Biarritz, and being in Biarritz with little to do, they naturally began going to the casino. They also decided that they were both too heavy and together went on a banana-and-milk diet. Whether it was the idleness or the overabundance of potassium, or the pit-of-the-stomach fear that they faced returning to Paris in debt, they began to see the casino—winning at it, anyway—as their salvation. As Bricktop

recalled, they went there even the night before they were scheduled to depart for Paris.

In Bricktop's recollection, "We won like crazy. I was at
baccarat and Mabel was at *chemin de fer*. For a gal who gambled
very little, Mabel was winning so fast she couldn't keep track.
She was a regular Nick the Greek. I quit playing to help her
count her winnings.

"We went back to the hotel suite, finally. It was a relief to
feel that we could go back to Paris in something resembling
style. I was really counting francs that season. We weren't there
a minute when Mabel said, 'Bricky, let's go back to the Casino.'

"I couldn't believe it. 'Mabel, you don't know what you're
talking about. Quit while you're ahead. . . .'

"Mabel went back anyway. Two or three hours later I
heard her coming back. I had been reading. I put out the light.
I waited until she was in bed before I hollered across the con-
necting bath to her room, 'Mabel, how did it go?' There was
a long pause. 'Forget it, Brick. Go to sleep.' Of course she had
lost everything.

"Fortunately, we were on one of those milk-and-banana
diets, so the twelve-hour train trip to Paris didn't kill us. At
the station Mabel started looking around for a porter. Then she
stopped. We didn't have the money to pay him. It was hard to
believe, but we hadn't a sou between us. We carried our own
bags to the taxi rack, and at Mabel's apartment the concierge
had to pick up the taxi fare."[34]

It was a struggle to open up Bricktop's that fall, and the
season was "spotty," to use Bricktop's term. Some nights the
club was less than half full. "People who never had a prayer of
getting into Bricktop's in the big years had no trouble getting
in now," Bricktop recalled. There were fewer parties, fewer
lavish tips, and both Bricktop and Mabel had to count their
francs. They began to wonder about the future of Bricktop's
and about their own futures, but both of them decided to hang
on as long as they possibly could. They did not have a lot of
other choices.

The following summer, 1934, they returned to Biarritz, or

more accurately to St. Jean-de-Luz, the resort town next to it. Bricktop rented space at the Yacht Club on the water, and it was there that she and Mabel first met Wallis Simpson, who had become the constant companion of the Prince of Wales. That winter, Lady Thelma Furness had been called back to the United States, and she'd asked her good friend Wallis to keep the Prince company. The South of France was all abuzz about the new relationship, but Mabel refused to join in the gossip. Privately, she and Bricktop agreed that Mrs. Simpson could not possibly be expecting to be Queen of England; otherwise, she would not treat the Prince in such a down-to-earth manner. According to Bricktop, "She was always saying, 'No, I don't think it's that way, boy. No, that's not right, boy.' If you wanted to become the Queen of England, would you call the future King 'boy'?"[35] Mabel would not then, and never would later, discuss the British royal family, other than to say nice things about them. "The Duke and Duchess of Windsor used to come in, and I got to know them," she told Whitney Balliet in 1982. "The Duke and Duchess of Kent came into Brick's, too, and the Duke and Duchess of York. The Duke of Kent was my favorite of the brothers—a very gentle man. And I loved the Duchess of York—Elizabeth, now the Queen Mother. She was a doll."[36] The British royalty, in particular the Prince of Wales, made Mabel's and Bricktop's month in St. Jean-de-Luz a happy time, when they didn't think about returning to Paris in the fall.

By the fall of 1934, Bricktop was doing some serious belt tightening. She and her husband, Peter Ducongé, had separated (they would never be divorced), and she decided to give up the villa they had owned in Bougival. She decided, too, not to try to reopen the club at 66 Rue Pigalle, for it was simply too large for the sparse clientele she and Mabel were attracting. Instead, she opened Bricktop's in a smaller space on the Rue Pigalle.

She and Mabel continued to welcome the British nobility. That autumn Prince George, now Duke of Kent, married Princess Marina of Greece, and at some point during the winter or spring of 1935 he and his bride went to Bricktop's. It happened that Paul Robeson and his wife, Essie, were also in the club that night, and Mabel and Bricktop were delighted by the stir that both men caused. Bricktop recalled many years later, ". . . the band started playing a dance tune, and Paul got up to dance with Essie, and the Duke got up to dance with Marina. When they met on the floor, they stopped—and since when royalty stops, everybody stops, all the dancers froze. Both Paul and the Duke were tall, but Paul was a little taller and had to look down on the Duke a bit. It's an image that has stayed in my mind all these years—everyone frozen in position on the dance floor and Paul looking down on the Duke.

"I was at the door, with Mabel at my side, and we both started crying. Mabel said, 'What are you crying about?' and I said it was because I was so proud of Paul Robeson. 'What are *you* crying about?' I wanted to know, and Mabel said it was because she was so proud of 'her Duke.' "[37]

There were few such proud moments at Bricktop's that season. More frequent were the sad and embarrassing moments when heretofore big spenders came by for a last farewell, and ordered a stinger instead of champagne, or when formerly wealthy patrons asked for the loan of a few francs. Everybody was broke, and that included Bricktop and Mabel. Suddenly finding themselves in the same predicament as the ordinary French of Montmartre, they became closer to them, and shared what they could with them. At Christmas, Mabel tried to lighten the mood with an eggnog recipe she had concocted from evaporated milk, but even that was in short supply. There were times when Mabel and Bricktop went hungry in order to pay the rent.

These financial straits had a more profound effect on Mabel than they did on Bricktop, who had family back in the United States and a sister, Blonzetta, in Chicago who had been highly successful in real estate. Asking her family for help would have been a last resort for Bricktop, but she did have that last resort. Mabel had no one to whom she felt she could turn, and it may have been at this time that, when she did have extra money, she began to hoard staples like dried beans and tinned milk, and when she began to sew her own gowns, which were as necessary as ever if she were to be a presentable entertainer.

By the fall of 1936, Bricktop realized there was no way she could reopen her club, and when her former headwaiter Jimmy Mussolini informed her that he was opening up a club of his own in Montparnasse and asked her and Mabel to work for him for a percentage, they accepted. And once they did, everyone began to call the place "Bricktop's." The Windsors and the Porters, Lady Mendl and the others who were still in Paris, followed Bricktop and Mabel to Jimmy's, and he was doing a good business by the spring of 1937. Apparently he believed he could continue to do a good business without paying Bricktop and Mabel a percentage, and he suggested that he pay them a flat salary instead. Mabel and Bricktop refused, and left Jimmy's.

They went next to the Big Apple, named after the dance of the time, a club that American singer Adelaide Hall, who had introduced "I Can't Give You Anything But Love" in *Blackbirds of 1928* and had starred in the Harlem Cotton Club's fall 1933 show, had opened with her husband. Once again, aficionados of Bricktop and Mabel called it "Bricktop's." Mabel stood when she performed there, stood in front of the Quintet du Hot Club de France, a group fronted by Stéphane Grappelly but which was built around gypsy guitarist Django Reinhardt. Perhaps that is why the Big Apple was, in the words of Julius Monk, *directoire artiste* at another club called Le Boeuf sur le Toit, "not much of a triumph." Mabel's forte was sitting and singing at tables.

Still, not a few patrons came especially to see Mabel. Julius Monk was among them. "I would absolutely scale boroughs, arrondissements, to get over to Bricky's to hear Mabel do 'How Deep Is the Ocean,' says Monk. "We [Mabel's aficionados] were like spawning salmon. I remember once I said to Mabel, 'My dear, you are the equivalent of a breast-feeding.' Which is true. Yes, everyone had a Mama fixation—Mother Courage plus

Earth. That was our own fantasy, you know. We created Mabel. She was there, for every single solitary soul and their singular fantasies, which was a remarkable gift. She animated the Empress's clothes."

Monk feels that by this time a certain competitiveness had arisen between Bricktop and Mabel. "You see, Bricktop had always been the principal of the ménage, and titular head of Bricky's, and then Mabel had her own following. It was very dangerous when someone would come in to hear Mabel, because Bricktop was a personality singer, you know, and did not have a formal singing voice in any sense of the word."

If the competitiveness was conscious in any way, that could have been due to the increasingly hard times for both women. That season, too, was spotty, and both Bricktop and Mabel were counting their francs. Bricktop often kept track of monies paid and monies owed. Her diary for 1937 contained the following notations:

    4/23—Mabel 500—6700
    4/29—Mabel 500—7200 [probably a reference to the total paid
        Mabel so far]
    5/19—Mabel cash 100
    6/9 —Mabel 200, Brick 250
    6/11—Mabel and I 500 each from L. B. Bill [possibly for a
        party or another club engagement][38]

In the fall of 1937 they went to work at a club run by a Madame Fricka and her husband. Once again, they worked on a percentage basis, and Bricktop was allowed to bring in musicians of her own choosing, among them Django Reinhardt and Stéphane Grappelly. The gypsy Django, whose skill on the guitar was not marred in the least when a fire in his caravan in November 1928 when he was nineteen had fused together the fourth and fifth of his fingers of his right, fret-board hand, was a capricious sort. He disliked working when he wasn't in the mood, and was as apt to go fishing as to show up for work. After a set, he often went off to a nearby club to visit friends, or play pool, and Mabel was always having to go out and look for him. Franklin D. Roosevelt, Jr., was a particular fan of Reinhardt's, and when he appeared and asked for him, some one had to go and find him. Mabel was very fond of Reinhardt and did not really mind her sometimes nightly searches, but even she became exasperated with him at times.[39] For his part, Reinhardt liked Mabel and wrote a song, "Mabel," which his Quintet du Hot Club de France recorded for Victor in 1937.

Although the French economy was improving somewhat, neither Mabel nor Bricktop could see a bright road ahead for the club business. The spur to the economy was a result of the increased talk of war—the government stepped up its manufacture of arms, which meant more jobs. The conscription of thousands of young Frenchmen meant at least that their families would be guaranteed an income. But club owners would see little of this income.

Talk of war became rampant, although Frenchmen and lovers of France who pooh-poohed the idea that France would ever be invaded were as numerous as those who painted frightening visions of German tanks rumbling down the Champs Elysées; at that time, many were still calling the conflict the "phony war." Neither Bricktop nor Mabel knew what to think.

Mabel went to London in late July–early August, probably to perform but also perhaps to see the Bouchers, her adopted family. She may have discussed with them what she ought to do, but if any decisions were made they had little effect on her professional schedule. When she returned to Paris, however, she apparently took a different apartment, no doubt smaller, as an economy measure. Bricktop noted in her diary on September 20, 1937, an address and telephone number for Mabel, and since she had worked with Mabel for seven years there was no reason for her to do so unless both had changed.

There were other changes in store. Mabel, for one, had finally decided that she had to start getting work on her own. In February 1938, she appeared at the Tushinski Theatre in

Amsterdam with Eddie South, an American-born violinist who was known for his concentration on tone and feeling—a style to which Mabel could easily relate. In early June she went to London again, and there recorded with Harry Roy's big band for EMI (Electric and Musical Industries). One of the cuts was "Black Minnie's Got the Blues" from the 1938 film *Everything Is Rhythm*. She was back in Paris by the middle of the month, for Bricktop noted in her diary that on June 18 she paid Mabel and "Cooper" five francs each. The Cooper referred to was Opal Cooper, the American singer and sometime banjo player whom Mabel was now seeing, and with whom she was apparently working on occasion, although not for much money. She left Paris again, briefly, for Bricktop recorded on July 7, 1938: "Mabel flew back. Started Boeuf."[40]

Le Boeuf sur le Toit had been in existence at one location or another in Paris since the early 1920s. It took its name, translated as "The Cow on the Roof," from a popular Brazilian tune, on which Darius Milhaud, one of the '20s avant-garde composers called Les Six, had based one of his pieces. In the early Twenties, when the club was on the Rue Boissy d'Anglais, it was a favorite gathering place for composers and writers, among them Erik Satie, Jean Cocteau, and René Clair. By the end of the decade, that group had drifted away, and Herbert Jacoby, owner of Le Boeuf, had moved it to Rue de Penthièvre, where it became popular among well-to-do and socially distinguished gays, remaining highly successful even after Herbert Jacoby left for New York to open a similar night club there. Julius Monk remembers that the Boeuf closed for the summer that year, but Monk had no trouble opening up a summer club in St. Tropez. "This was in 1937 and it was in that tower that you see in *La Cage* [*aux Folles*], that seventeenth-century tower—with Garland Wilson, the black pianist, and Lutie Belle Carlyle." The following summer, however, the club remained open in Paris, possibly because it could boast Mabel Mercer as its chief attraction. Toward the end of the summer Mabel went to the South of France, where Joe Carstairs first saw her.

Marion Barbara Carstairs had family money and connections on both sides of the Atlantic. "My whole family are Americans, but I am British," she says. "My father was in the Black
Watch in the Indian Army. My mother was married four times,
and I was [the issue of] the first. My grandfather's name was
Bostwick and he worked for the oil companies [he was a major
shareholder in Standard Oil of New Jersey]." But she was not
your usual international socialite. She preferred the initials M.B.
to Marion Barbara, when she had to use her real name, but
always referred to herself as Joe. She'd made her own fame and
fortune racing speedboats. "I met Mabel Mercer in the South
of France, with Marlene Dietrich. It was outside of Cannes, a
party, and she was singing there. She was very popular at the
time. I met her and I thought she was a very great lady and
had a marvelous voice. She was very proper, you know, just
the opposite to me."

What the two women had in common, and one basis for
their instant friendship, was that they were the same age. "She
was born the same year as I was. She was about the third or
fourth of February, and I was the first. But she always seemed
much older than me. I always thought of her as a great lady.
We all thought that. She always behaved like that. She didn't
behave young at all."

There had been little in Mabel's life to feel young about,
and by the time she met Joe Carstairs she was facing a major
crisis. In the summer of 1938 there was a real question as to
whether she might not soon be entertaining Nazis, and as Joe
Carstairs puts it, "The Germans wouldn't have cared for her at
all." By the end of August an ominous quiet had descended on
Paris. Electricians who hadn't been mobilized in the war effort
tried to dim the streetlamps. Methylene blue paint was daubed
on the windows of railroad stations and corner cafés. Often,
the only sound seemed to be that of radios blaring out recorded
repetitions of Premier Edouard Daladier's speech stating that
France, this time, would stand firm and honor its promises. On
September 3, 1938, war was declared, and when Mabel returned
to Paris, she saw sights she had never imagined—concierges

taping up windows and sealing air-raid shelters, workers painting street crossings white so they could be seen in a blackout,
and shuttered shops. There were announcements that markets
would be open only in the daytime, that Parisians were urged
to leave the city, that henceforth the newspaper coverage of the
war would be censored.

The Paris Mabel loved seemed to be changing overnight.
Many among the American colonies, black and white, had already left, urged to do so by the American consul, who informed them that as foreigners they would be interned by the
Germans. Among the blacks, Charlie Lewis and Arthur Briggs
were still around, as was Opal Cooper, who had not been back
to the United States in more than twenty years and did not
relish returning. Among the whites, there were still a well-to-
do few who urged both Mabel and Bricktop to leave Paris, at
least for a while. Among those who pressed Mabel was Joe
Carstairs, who urged her to go to New York and offered to
finance her trip. Mabel had never had the remotest idea of going
to the United States.

It was one of the most difficult decisions she had ever made,
and she worried over it for weeks before she made her choice.
Among the points in favor of making the trip were the specter
of a Paris under blue light with the stomping boots of Nazi
regiments in the dark streets and swarms of refugees in public
places and, perhaps most of all, her awareness that her mother
was in the United States, somewhere (Mabel still had a deep
longing to see her mother). Among the points against it were
leaving the beloved Paris that had once been, her cozy apartment
filled with books and her own pastel drawings, and her friends,
especially Opal Cooper and Bricktop. "She was in a terrible
mess," says Carstairs. "She wouldn't come. She was one of
those diehards. She had a cat, and she didn't want to leave the
cat or the apartment, and it got iffy. I mean, it got pretty bloody
awful. And I finally got her to leave. She came on the *Queen
Mary*, the old *Queen Mary*, and it was the day before they took
the lights off the shipping coming across the Atlantic."

Mabel left in October 1938, left her apartment, her beloved

little cat, her friends, and the Paris she had loved—all for what she could only have regarded as the dangerous unknown.

Bricktop chose to listen to those who urged her to remain in Paris, among them Lady Mendl and the Duchess of Windsor. She would remain in Paris almost exactly one year after Mabel left, waiting until the last possible moment and making her decision only after the Nazis invaded Poland in August 1939. She missed Mabel deeply, and was constantly reminded of her close friend after she took over Mabel's apartment with its books and paintings and all around the evidence of Mabel's eccentric manner of organization. One of the entries in Bricktop's diary for 1939 reads: "Mabels tax papers top drawer under spoons."[41]

CHAPTER

III

WANDERING CHANTEUSE

WHEN MABEL STEPPED off the *Queen Mary* in New York that fall of 1938, awaiting her on the dock was her mother. Mabel had not seen her since she was a child. They had corresponded over the years, and she had written to let her mother know that she was coming. But she had no way of knowing whether or not her mother would show up. What took place between the two women is not known, for Mabel did not talk about it. It may have been then that her mother told her that she had a new American husband who knew nothing about Mabel, and could not know, for he would not have accepted a half-black step-daughter. Whatever the two women talked about, their meeting was brief but had a tremendous emotional impact on Mabel.

"I was waiting on the thirty-second floor of the Pierre Hotel," says Bart Howard, who was then twenty-three years old and newly arrived in New York to make his fortune as a piano player and songwriter. "I was in Joe Carstairs's suite. Someone, maybe it was Tim Brook, Joe's secretary, had gone to the dock to meet [Mabel]. She came in, and I was introduced. Joe was there, Tim was there, and I don't remember who else might have been there. I noticed she was teary. She was very well dressed and looked very smart and not heavy (but you could tell she would be), and she was teary. I didn't know why. Later, I asked why and was told that on the dock was her mother, whom she hadn't seen for thirty years. . . . I guess she had not told her present husband [about Mabel]. She lived up near Greenwood Lake in New York. She was there, saw Mabel, and then went back to where she came from, and Mabel I guess was eight years old when she had seen her mother last, and that's why she was teary. To have just seen her mother for a minute and then to have her disappear. . . . Or at least that's what I was told."

Mabel had no way of knowing, although she was soon to find out, that she might have had a second emotionally laden experience before she even reached Joe Carstairs's suite at the Pierre. "In those days," says Howard, "there was some talk about whether they would somehow stop us from taking her up in the elevator. We decided we would do it anyway, and we just brought her up in the elevator and there was no difficulty. But those were the days when there could have been trouble."

The young Howard, not long out of Iowa, was in rarefied company. "When I was planted in New York in 1937, somebody took me to a hotel that was housing all the British actors who were coming over to work in places, so I got to be very good friends with so many of the English. And as a result I met a man who was an author—and I was trying to be a songwriter—and I needed a lyricist and we thought we were going to do some work after that. And he turned out to be very much looked after by a rich woman named Joe Carstairs, so he kept telling her about me, and one day I went to meet her. She

thought I had very good manners and played the piano well
and was 'personable,' and she took me under her wing, too. I
had a little money, but she saw to it that I wasn't going to
starve to death for the rest of my life. She has helped a lot of
people over the years—I don't know how many college tuitions
she's paid.

"I had heard a record of Mabel's that Marlene [Dietrich]
had made—'You Better Go Now'/'The Folks Who Live on the
Hill.' She had a high soprano voice, which most people now
wouldn't believe. It was a sweet rendition, and I'd heard nothing
but wonderful things about Mabel. I liked her immediately, and
she liked me. I think I was the first friend that Mabel made in
this country."

There was no question at all about whether or not Mabel
would be able to stay at the Pierre, or anywhere else downtown
for that matter. That very night, Mabel went up to Harlem.
"I'm not sure where she stayed," says Howard. "She might
have gone to stay with [black singer] Jimmy Daniels." Not long
afterward, Mabel began to stay with a friend called Sadie at
2040 Seventh Avenue, and Harlem remained her home base
during the time she was in New York. She could perform
downtown, but she had to live uptown, a situation she did
not like.

Mabel was far from certain about her future. She had a
visitor's visa only and did not know the procedure for becoming
a permanent resident; for that matter, she was unsure whether
she wanted to be a permanent resident in New York, her first
impression of which was hardly favorable: it had none of the
human scale and gardenlike quality of Montmartre, and in the
late 1930s was hardly a bastion of racial enlightenment.

"With all due respect," she told William Livingstone, "I
thought it was *frightfully* strange. . . . The buildings were like
monolithic gravestones, and it was all so different. And for *me*
it was different for other reasons. I could never get over the
fact that I couldn't go here or couldn't go there. I couldn't
understand why not."[1]

Joe Carstairs recalls, "There was a thing she could not stand, and that was whenever she went anywhere she was pointed out and called black, or whatever. I think it upset her. In America, that was so—during that time. She was very conscious of it, and when a group of us would take her out to dinner, she would say, 'Let me tell you where I can go.' "

The world of New York society was also considerably different from that of Paris, although in some respects it was the same. The Depression notwithstanding, New York café society was as glamorous and opulent as Paris night life had been in the golden days. One reason, no doubt, was that the war had forced the millionaires to stay at home; denied the opportunity to spend their money in Paris and Biarritz and like places, they were constrained to spend it in New York. Wrote Lucius Beebe in *Hearst's International–Cosmopolitan* in the spring of 1937, "Never before, probably, has New York been snowed under by such a blizzard of money as is now drifting through its streets, piling up at its night clubs and in the ateliers of its court jewelers, furriers, couturiers and luxury tradesmen. Mink coats at forty thousand dollars have become commonplace. There is a rare perfume on the market priced—and selling—at five hundred dollars for an ounce flask. There is a positive shortage of matched sables and chinchilla; diamond boutonnieres for men are being passed over the counter at ten thousand dollars a copy; waiter captains are playing the market again, and it's possible for two to dine at the Colony and have very little change out of a half-century banknote."[2]

Mabel was no stranger to many of the names in the society pages—she had entertained half of these lights at Bricktop's. Noel Coward annually spent twelve weeks in New York, frequenting few nightclubs but attending numerous private parties. Cole Porter, when he was in town, Monty Woolley, and Ernest Hemingway all favored "21." Elsa Maxwell was often in residence at the Colony, when she wasn't throwing extravagant costume balls, like her "Barnyard Frolic" at the Starlight Roof of the Waldorf-Astoria, for which Cleveland millionaire Leonard Hanna, a onetime regular at Bricktop's, imported a genuine Ohio hog caller. Rivaling Maxwell as a party-giver was Mrs. Cobina Wright, the typical turnout at whose affairs would include Peggy Fears, Dwight Fiske, and Tallulah Bankhead. There were assorted royalty in the New York café society of the late 1930s, and plenty of members of the Social Register. But the Depression had shattered the social order of New York, and café society was now an amalgam of debutantes, show business types, nobodies, artists, and gossip columnists. As Lucius Beebe noted, "The cafe society of modern New York is infinitely more democratic, more open to achievement, than was the older social order. The requirements for membership in it are primarily those of professional success, personal distinction and willingness to subscribe to only the vaguest of formal codes. Almost anybody with something to offer stands an excellent chance of becoming somebody in cafe society."[3]

Perhaps sensing that New York was fertile ground for classy night spots, Herbert Jacoby, former assistant manager of Le Boeuf sur le Toit in Montparnasse, had opened Le Ruban Bleu at 4 East 56th Street that year. According to Julius Monk, the name referred to an area on the coast of Normandy. Like Le Boeuf, it also catered primarily to a gay clientele, but only the best, as Bricktop liked to put it. The club boasted excellent entertainment, and Mabel opened there a couple of weeks after she arrived.

Bart Howard was there for her opening night, along with Joe Carstairs and Tim Brook. Marlene Dietrich was at the next table, with Clifton Webb. "In the meantime, Mabel had come back to the Pierre," says Bart Howard, "and I had a song called 'If You Leave Paris,' which was written at this time when Paris was just about to go. The lyric was written by an Englishman, and Marlene suggested that Mabel sing that song when she opened at Le Ruban Bleu. So, that opening night, Mabel sang the first song I ever had sung in New York, and it became part of her repertoire right away."

Asked in 1975 by William Livingstone to recall who else

was singing at Le Ruban Bleu when she arrived, Mabel reflected for a moment and said, "There was Elsie Houston. She had a beautiful voice, not really a classical voice, but it had great tenderness, and when she sang those fados [Portuguese folk songs] she was marvelous. It was 1938 and Greta Keller came that year. And there was a wonderful couple who were in [Leonard] Sillman's first *New Faces*; she was a very dark girl with a smile that lit up the room. I *cannot* remember her name. She used to sing 'I'm the Prettiest Piece in Greece,'" so you know they were good songs! Then a French lady came (she was very funny), and Richard Dyer-Bennett, and a girl called Olga something, an Argentine girl, and Julius Monk, who was the sort of master of ceremonies."[4]

When Julius Monk read that article, "I wrote to Mabel instantly. There was no harm done, but I just wrote in a jolly, chatty way, 'Mabel, we've never worked together at Le Ruban Bleu. No wonder you didn't quite know what I was doing there! And the girl was Cuban—Graziella Parragar—and the couple from *New Faces* (1935 or 1934) was Billy and Cliff—the girl was Billy Haywood and the pianist was Cliff Allen.' "

Billed as "Mabel Mercer, formerly of Bricktop's, Paris," and seeing familiar faces in the club every night, Mabel began to feel at home, and although she still failed to understand the strict racial lines in the city, New York began to grow on her.

Mabel remained at Le Ruban Bleu for six months, which wasn't a bad first engagement for a newcomer. But bookings after that were spotty, and Mabel lived a hand-to-mouth existence. When Bricktop arrived in New York in late November 1939, having at last decided that Paris was not safe for her, she immediately looked up Mabel. Had Mabel then been flush, Bricktop would have asked her for a loan, but as Bricktop recalled, "She wasn't working at the time and so couldn't help me out in that way."

Mabel couldn't seem to find a steady engagement, although she performed here and there on occasion. In between engagements, she depended greatly on friends, among them Jimmy

Daniels, Bart Howard, and Joe Carstairs. She received moral support, but no money, from Bart Howard. "I went to hear her a lot. People would take me there. In those days as long as I could pay the taxi fare, I thought I was doing my bit, you know. And black tie—of course, being a musician, that was the best suit I had so I always looked good. And I got to know Mabel quite well. I was writing, but she didn't do any more of my songs at that time." Mabel also received moral support, but no money, from Bricktop, who was having a tough time herself in New York.

Bricktop had hoped to be able to find a New York spot where she could recreate Bricktop's, but she also realized that New York was not Paris: "I wasn't going to be able to rent a little place, buy a few bottles of champagne, and open up Bricktop's.

"I'd seen the New York clubs—the jazz spots on 52nd Street, the big floor-show places like the Latin Quarter and the Copacabana, the tiny East Side bistros and Greenwich Village spots. They had nothing in common with the intimate clubs of Paris. They didn't attract a Bricktop's crowd. My clients went to the Stork Club, El Morocco, the Colony, and '21.' Even if I'd wanted to, and I didn't, I couldn't manage their kind of operation—and I'm not just talking about expenses and size. These were segregated clubs. . . ."[5]

Bricktop had had her own taste of segregation, New York style, when Cole Porter had hosted a welcoming party for her at his Waldorf Towers apartment; she had asked the receptionist in the lobby for Porter's apartment and "he looked at me as if he'd never seen a Negro woman before." Bricktop noticed that even some old friends treated her differently now that she was in New York; they were more standoffish and very curious about how she liked being (a Negro) in America. She got the opportunity to have her own room at Jimmy Savini's club on East 56th Street, but she and Savini soon had a falling-out over her habit of buying drinks for the customers. She then went to the Coq Rouge and a Bricktop's room, but the strange patrons who had been lured there primarily by the publicity attendant to the opening of the room seemed to resent her style. "And," said Bricktop, "that was *before* they had heard me sing."[6] She didn't attract enough business, and was asked to leave the club. In short, Bricktop was in no position to help Mabel.

What made matters worse for Mabel was that she began to suffer seriously from tonsilitis. She'd been bothered by sore throats often. Back in Paris, she could attribute it to the dampness of the winters or to cigar smoke in the clubs, until she put a stop to that. In New York, she could blame her throat problems on the smog, or the oppressive humidity of the summertime. When informed that she needed to have her tonsils removed, she despaired for a time, for there was no guarantee that her singing voice would not be affected. That voice, cautious though it was, was all she had. Still, she had no choice but to go through with the operation.

Coincidentally, Bart Howard also had a tonsilectomy at the same time as Mabel did. "They were a bit old to have tonsilectomies, and in those days it was rather painful and could be dangerous," says Joe Carstairs. "It was done at Eye, Ear, Nose & Throat Hospital, I imagine, because I knew a doctor there. They came and recuperated at the hotel where I was. She and Bart had rooms apart and drank liquids and ate ice cream until they got better. It was about two weeks. If the people at the hotel objected [to Mabel's staying there], they didn't tell me. I was very overpowering. I said, 'She's going to stay here, and that's that.' After all, you don't stand for any of that shit."

Once her recuperation was complete, Mabel's voice returned to its earlier form. "Her voice came back, and she was singing damn well, jolly well," says Joe Carstairs. But Mabel still wasn't getting steady work, and when Carstairs invited her to her private island in the Bahamas, Mabel was delighted to accept.

The island was called Whale Key. "It was in the middle of the Atlantic," says Carstairs. "I got that after the racing. I was there with a whole bunch of chaps, and we were working. I was actually doing agriculture for HRH—Windsor."

The Duke of Windsor had accepted an appointment as Governor of the Bahamas—under some duress, since he was well aware that the appointment had been tendered because it was felt that his continued presence in Paris when so much of the Continent was in enemy hands was an embarrassment to England. Says Carstairs, "They sent him down there because they didn't know what to do with him, and I got to know the Duchess very well." Mabel didn't care why he was there; she just enjoyed the idea of being where the Windsors were again.

"The island was very rough and wild," says Carstairs. Mabel loved it. "She used to walk around and plant things. Matter of fact, she planted a couple of trees. She used to walk around with a basket over her head and a shovel—she was very strong, you know. We all worked jolly hard."

And if the naturalness of the island were not enough to make the island seem like paradise to Mabel, it also had a church. "We had a very nice little church on the hill," says Carstairs, "and we allowed everybody in it. I'm Church of England, but I didn't pay any attention to that. Anybody could be in that church, it didn't belong to any sect. We had the Jumpers—we used to call them Jumpers, they made a lot of noise and jumped around a bit—and the Fifth Day Adventists. It was looked upon as rather dreadful, but I don't believe in 'secticism.'"

Not long after that first visit, Mabel went to the Bahamas on a professional basis, to play a season there with Bart Howard as her accompanist. Julius Monk remembers that Joe Carstairs held a gala going-away party for herself, Mabel, and Bart Howard, in her suite at the Pierre Hotel. Monk attended the party —"her sort of *despedida*": "They left within forty-eight hours." The steamship journey was one long party, and Mabel looked forward to being again surrounded by British culture, to seeing her Duke of Windsor, and to be doing *something* instead of just marking time and wondering where her next engagement was coming from.

59

"It was 1940 when I went down," says Howard, "and I went to work with her over in Nassau—Paul Mears's place over the hill. She knew him from Paris. He lived with a white girl, his dancing partner, on the same floor of the hotel with us when Mabel and I had two rooms on the front and they had two rooms on the back. We all ate together. Mabel and I worked there the winter. We'd do one show in the big show, which was at midnight or something, and at two o'clock we opened a bar in the same building, and we sang until eight o'clock in the morning. And I began writing songs and Mabel started using them. We used to visit Joe Carstairs on her island, and plant bougainvillea. Eventually, the season ended, or whatever, so I went back to New York. She stayed, of course."

At the time, there was no "of course" about it. Mabel had had every intention of returning to New York, but there was the small matter of the reentry permit that Mabel, who never was very good at things like taxes and permits, was supposed to have obtained. "Apparently, she had neglected to get a reentry permit," says Bart Howard. "She was stuck."

Unwilling to take advantage of Joe Carstairs's hospitality any longer, Mabel struck out on her own. "The Duke and Duchess of Windsor sponsored her a lot," says Howard. Says Carstairs, "Mabel used to go a great deal and sing for them in the great house in Nassau—they liked her very much."

Among the newspaper clippings Mabel kept is this one from a Nassau paper dated Tuesday, June 24, 1941:

HERE AND THERE
GOVERNOR AND DUCHESS ATTEND
RED CROSS DANCE

The dance given by Government House employees at the Silver Slipper last night in aid of the Red Cross Fund was well attended and will make a profit of over £40.

His Royal Highness the Governor and the Duchess of Windsor, accompanied by Major Gray-Philips, Captain and Mrs. George Wood, Capt. and Mrs. Vyvyan Drury and Capt.

Alistair Mackintosh, arrived at about 11 p.m. They were received by the Committee and conducted to a special box provided for the party.

An address of welcome was made by the Hon. A.F. Adderly to which His Royal Highness replied, and the Duchess also said a few words about the Red Cross, thanking those responsible for this effort.

Soon after their arrival an electrical storm developed and Miss Mabel Mercier [sic] kindly filled in this interval with a few songs. Miss Mercier has often sung for the royal party at private functions.

Music was provided by Rudy Williams and his orchestra and His Royal Highness and the Duchess, who remained for nearly an hour, joined the dancers on the floor.[7]

There is a story that Mabel, being "colored," had to look for work in the colored section of Nassau. According to this story, she made history there by being the first entertainer whom the white population would "cross the tracks" to hear.[8] Joe Carstairs disputes this story, however: "I was rather political in those days, and I don't remember anything like that at all." There is no question, however, that Mabel was popular in the Bahamas; the favorite songs she sang at the time were "Mandy" and "Dear Dorothy Dix, I'm in an Awful Fix."[9]

"She performed with Paul and Poppy Mears," says Julius Monk. "They had been with Josephine Baker at the Folies Bergère in Paris, and they were very exciting. It was near nudity that they did at the time. They had a club, I believe in Nassau."

Bart Howard returned to the Bahamas in 1941 to visit Joe Carstairs and spend some time on Whale Key. "Mabel was in Nassau. There was a big fair about to go on there, and Miss Carstairs had an exhibit, which I helped build. She had a large yacht, and she wanted the Windsors to see this yacht of hers, so we went over to Nassau and anchored way out from the land. The Windsors were going to come out to the yacht and visit her. I wanted to see Mabel, but I couldn't get to the land from the yacht without commandeering a launch, which I was reluctant to do. I was sure I was going to see Mabel at the fair, but that was a very busy time for me, helping Joe. Mabel never appeared and I went back to the boat. I never did get to see Mabel, which later she held against me. It was very hard for me. She forgave me, but I didn't have the guts to say I had to go to lunch and go see Joe.

"I didn't even get to see the Windsors, because the afternoon they were to come to the yacht I had to take a plane out. I was going back to the States to join the army, and I was in the army for five years."

By this time the Japanese had bombed Pearl Harbor and the United States had entered World War II. Mabel's chances of getting back to the United States became even more dismal, for not only did she not have the proper papers, she was an alien in wartime. All she could do was hope for some break and in the meantime remain as current as she could with the latest music. Among the pieces she heard that struck her fancy were Alec Wilder's octets. Loonis McGlohon, who knew her well in her later years, recalls, "These are little curious pieces that are a blend of jazz and classical music. They were recorded in 1938. They were little 2 1/2-, 3-, 3 1/2-minute pieces done by a small chamber ensemble—well, an octet—oboe, woodwinds, harpsichord, drums, and bass—like a jazz rhythm section with classical writing on top, with very provocative titles like 'His First Long Pants' and 'The House Detective Registers.' Mabel heard this music in the Bahamas, and she said, 'I must go to New York and meet the man who wrote this music.'" But there seemed no way for Mabel to get back to New York until Kelsey Pharr came to her rescue.

Pharr was an American, born in Florida and of a well-to-do Southern black family. "They were Southern black aristocrats," says the actress Rosetta LeNoire, who met Pharr not long after he arrived in New York to seek his fortune. "Kelsey was such a gentleman, and when you met his father you knew why. He was really one of the old-time aristocratic black gentlemen. When he'd come up to New York, we all knew we were gonna eat well."

LeNoire and Pharr were fresh from the road tour of *The Hot Mikado*, the Mike Todd production starring Bill "Bojangles" Robinson that had been such a smash hit on Broadway and later at the 1939 World's Fair. "Frances Brock and I were two of the Three Little Maids in the show," says LeNoire, and it was through Frances that I met Kelsey. We were all in *The Hot Mikado*, and then we were all in *Head of the Family*, written by Mr. George Norford. He and Frannie and I became good friends. Then Kelsey and some of the guys from *The Hot Mikado* formed the Delta Rhythm Boys, and I heard that Kelsey had a chance to go to Europe or somewhere, and when he came back he told us he was married!"

In his travels, Pharr had gotten to Nassau and met Mabel, and Mabel had confided in him her predicament. She was a woman without a country, unable to return to England or France because of the war, unable to return to the United States because of visa problems. Whether she asked Pharr to marry her, or whether he made the offer, the marriage was the answer to Mabel's dilemma. Wed to an American, she would be able to return to the United States. Says Joe Carstairs, "All those so-called English people did that, because they couldn't take papers out or work or anything. She married Pharr just to get into the country. He was much younger than she. Apparently, he was a very nice, accommodating fellow, and I always remember his name, Pharr, because I'm very much seagoing, and Pharr means lighthouse."

The story goes that the two interrupted the Duke of Windsor's golf game to get his signature on an emergency marriage license, and within a week Mabel was in New York.[10]

According to Mabel Mercer legend, she and Kelsey Pharr, who was openly homosexual, barely saw one another after the official ceremony. Rosetta LeNoire remembers differently. "When Kelsey told me he was married to Mabel Mercer, I had not heard of her," she recalls. "He told me she was a very successful singer and that she was quite celebrated in Europe. She was pretty well known, at least among black people, because in those days she was doing so much better than the rest of them. The aristocracy, too, was very, very taken with her, like Bobby Short here.

"When she arrived in New York, we gave a welcome dinner for her. Frannie and I got our little pennies together. Kelsey was living on 110th Street at the time, and his landlady had a very large apartment facing the park—that was an elite section, on 110th between Lenox and Seventh Avenues in those days—and she let us have her dining room and use her kitchen. Given what we could afford, we had a nice dinner for Mabel.

"She was young then, but she came across as a genuine lady—soft-spoken, well-spoken—and if she didn't know something she would tell you in the nicest way, and if she did she could convey it and explain it to you with such quiet, secure warmth. And in the time that I knew her, Mabel Mercer did not change one single bit.

"I was on the road a lot—had to be in order to work—and I heard that she and Kelsey had somewhat agreed to go their separate ways, but with the greatest of fondness and friendship. And in case of emergency, they called on each other, and they were always right there. Both of them were always that way. Yes, he was much, much younger than she was; but he had great mental maturity, and they had great respect for each other."

In Will Craik's recollection, Mabel went to Florida to meet Pharr's parents soon after she and her new husband arrived in the United States. It is also probable that Mabel stayed with Pharr, or in his rooms, for a time. But he soon went back on the road with the Delta Rhythm Boys, and Mabel, her way to America having been lighted by the beacon, Kelsey Pharr, had to make it on her own.

Julius Monk feels that her voice had begun to change by this time, and attributed it to the tonsilectomy. "Mabel had begun losing her sense of pitch by the time she returned, which I am assured can often happen when surgery is done with a knife." By that time Monk had himself arrived in New York from Europe to take over the duties of *directoire artiste* at Le

Ruban Bleu. "Mabel in the thirties was a soprano, a mezzo, and you can hear this on the Liberty Music Shop label—the records still exist. Mabel does 'Summertime' with the obbligato, and things of this sort, and you think, what a perfectly charming and enchanting voice, but not that arresting, you know. After the surgery, she became a diseuse."

Others believe that the change in her voice was simply due to her age—she was now in her early forties. Whether she was bothered by the change or not, Mabel really had no alternative but to continue singing. She had no other marketable skills to speak of. No surgeon's knife had removed her feeling for a lyric, or her highly visual presentation of a song. She simply adjusted her new voice to her presentation, and no doubt thanked providence that she had not succeeded in becoming a concert mezzo-soprano as she once had hoped.

She and Bricktop got back together briefly, on the famed West 52nd Street, which by the early 1940s was a music mecca, particularly for jazz musicians and singers and their followers. The block between Fifth and Sixth avenues was lined primarily by five-story brownstones that had until the early Twenties housed the Rhinelanders, the Iselins, the Wagstaffs, Mrs. S. Stanwood Menken, and Bernard M. Baruch. As these families had made their fortunes they had moved to more fashionable neighborhoods, leaving the brownstones as prime locations for illicit entertainments. During Prohibition the operators of speakeasies discovered that West 52nd Street was a perfect location—near the center of things, but lined with quiet exteriors behind which they could hide. And of course the basements were ready-made for secret liquor cellars. When liquor was illegal in the United States, West 52nd Street housed some of the most outstanding speakeasies in America, including Leon & Eddie's and Jack and Charlie's "21." In fact, later on their illegal origins were boasted of as if that were tantamount to coming over on the *Mayflower*.

After Prohibition's repeal, many of the former speakeasies metamorphosed into hot-jazz clubs, and 52nd Street became

New York's answer to Bourbon Street and Beale Street, or as Arnold Shaw put it in *The Street That Never Slept*, America's Montmartre. The long, low, narrow rooms could not accommodate more than a small combo on their tiny stages, and so they were ideal for jazz. The Onyx Club seems to have begun this particular incarnation of West 52nd Street—it was there that the musicians from the nearby NBC and CBS studios came after rehearsals and broadcasts. Lennie Hayton (who later married Lena Horne), Paul Whiteman, the Dorsey brothers, Benny Goodman, Glenn Miller, Artie Shaw, Johnny Mercer, and many more came to regard the Onyx as home until it got too popular. They then chipped in and, led by Hayton, opened the Famous Door nearby. In the summer of 1938, the Famous Door played host to Count Basie's big band, and that memorable engagement was followed by equally successful gigs for Woody Herman's and Charlie Barnet's bands. Meanwhile, at Kelly's Stable on the more westerly block of 52nd Street, between Sixth and Seventh avenues, Billie Holiday, who had flopped at both the Onyx and the Famous Door, began to build a following. By 1939 Coleman Hawkins was packing the Stable nightly.

In Mabel's absence, Bricktop had played "limited engagements" at a couple of West 52nd Street clubs—limited, because after a short time she was asked to leave—before finding at last in 1941 a steady berth at Cerutti's on Madison Avenue, where she stayed for two years. Not long after Mabel returned to New York, Bricktop had been able to make a deal with the owners of the Three Deuces on West 52nd Street that would allow her to operate her own room. ". . . Mabel wasn't working," said Bricktop, "and it occurred to me that maybe the two of us could re-create Bricktop's. When I asked Mabel if she wanted to work for me there, she said, 'Yes, sure,' and we teamed up again briefly."[11]

It was just like old times for the two troupers. The idea of seeing Bricktop and Mabel Mercer together again attracted not a few of the patrons from the Paris days, not to mention a number of people who'd only heard about Bricktop's in the golden days of Paris. Bricktop especially enjoyed taking taxicabs with Mabel when they went home to Harlem at night: "Mabel got more elegant and that British accent became crisper as the night wore on, and it was sheer joy to hear her put New York's cranky cab drivers in their place."[12]

Unfortunately, the two were not long at the Three Deuces. As Bricktop recalled, the problem was a long-standing feud between one of the owners of the club and a friend of hers named Nigger Nate Raymond, a white man who had been a friend of the gambler Arnold Rothstein. They moved on to the Onyx Club at 52 West 52nd Street, the daddy of the swing spots founded in 1930 by Joe Helbock and the home-away-from-home for musicians like Benny Goodman and the Dorsey brothers. With the repeal of Prohibition, Helbock had inaugurated a formal music policy. He had also moved the club three times. Mabel and Bricktop opened the third Onyx Club in late June 1942.

"Those familiar with 52nd Street, or Night Club Row, will be surprised to find that the new Onyx Club is situated on the north, or non-jive, side of the thoroughfare," wrote Malcolm Johnson in the *New York Sun*. "It deals heavily in intimate atmosphere—the kind of little place where one may drop in for a drink or two, listen to the entertainment and drift on. The featured entertainment consists of two colored vocalists, Bricktop and Mabel Mercer. The latter, who has been heard at the Ruban Bleu, among other spots, has an attractive voice which she uses to advantage in singing songs of the nostalgic genre.

"Bricktop is a suave, hefty Harlem girl who went to Paris and was popular there for some years, but whose success since her return here, a few seasons back, has been only moderate. She has, however, a wide acquaintance among the play-boy and play-girl set of another era—or whatever is left of that set. Bricktop specializes in what are called smart or sophisticated lyrics. . . . If you like an atmosphere that is definitely intimate and informal and laboriously chic, the Onyx will probably fill the bill."[13]

It was at this club that publicist Eddie Jaffe first met Brick-top and Mabel. "I was the leading column-feeder," says Jaffe. "I would write for Winchell, Kilgallen, Leonard Lyons, Danton Walker, Earl Wilson, Robert Sylvester. Just getting things in those places would get you all the coverage you needed. My job on West 52nd Street was to show up at a club a couple nights a week and say who was there."

The emphasis on Bricktop in the Malcolm Johnson article for the *Sun* does not surprise Jaffe, who did publicity for the clubs for many years. "Mabel was always very remote, she was never aggressive in any way. She never did anything to promote herself—I don't think she ever spoke to me about publicity. If something was in the paper, I don't think she ever mentioned it. Bricktop, on the other hand, was very aggressive—what are you doing for me? I remember Bricktop doing all the talking —I don't think Mabel said a word!"

The Onyx Club was across the street from one called Tony's, which had in residence a pianist named Cy Walter. Born Cyril F. Walter in Minneapolis in 1915, Cy had learned music from his mother, a piano teacher, although he preferred to say that he was " 'osmosized' into it more than learned it."[14] He'd arrived in New York in 1934 to work with Eddie Lane's orchestra; after four years with Lane, he had opened at Le Ruban Bleu, where Mabel first heard him and was struck by his emphasis on show tunes of the late Twenties and Thirties, obscure melodies, and timeless tunes that had somehow been lost in the shuffle. He'd left Le Ruban Bleu shortly thereafter, and Mabel had tried to keep in touch, although her own travels had sometimes gotten in the way. He played the Algonquin and the Martinique and briefly had his own club, Cy Walter's Night Cap, before going to Tony's.

He was modest and understated, as was Mabel, and had a quiet, deprecating sense of humor, as did Mabel. Once asked how many drunks he'd seen in his many years as a cocktail pianist, Walter said, "I'll never forget the guy who came in one night and asked me to play the first act of Wagner's *Götterdäm-*

merung. "I told him I only knew the last act and he said, 'O.K. Play 'Stars and Stripes Forever.' Then I went to the keyboard and played 'Easter Parade.' "[15] Although Walter was some fifteen years Mabel's junior, Bricktop recalled that ". . . Mabel had a thing going with the piano player, Cy. She would run back and forth . . . [to] Tony's. . . ." Bricktop had no problem with that; Mabel's personal life was her own. But Mabel apparently grew to like Tony's. Recalled Bricktop, ". . . one day she said to me, 'Bricky, Cy has to go into the army, and Tony and Cy want to know if you'd mind if I went over to Tony's to work.'

"I said, 'No, go ahead,' and Mabel went to work at Tony's. She was there for seven years, and that's where she made her *big* reputation, just sitting and singing."[16]

Not long afterward, Bricktop also left the Onyx. She could not seem to make it on Swing Street. Nor was she successful in the other New York clubs where she appeared later. The tone of the *New York Sun* article is indicative of what Bricktop, for one, was up against. Her particular audience was "of another era." In 1944 she decided she'd had enough of New York and, with a stake provided by tobacco heiress Doris Duke, relocated to Mexico City, where she was very successful for several years. Coincidentally, not long before she moved to that highly Catholic city, Bricktop converted to Catholicism, a step that Mabel Mercer wholeheartedly endorsed.

While they still enjoyed a warm friendship, and took at least one trip to Joe Carstairs's island together during this time, the years in New York were hard on the relationship between Mabel Mercer and Bricktop. The friendly competition of the later Paris years became less friendly in New York—not because the two women encouraged it, but because Mabel's fans did. For all her problems, Mabel managed to carve out a niche of sorts for herself in New York—a niche that eluded Bricktop. As she watched Mabel's star rise and her own fall, Bricktop felt more and more often constrained to remind the world that it was she who had made Mabel Mercer a star. For her part, Mabel was always quick to remind her fans that she had gotten her start at Bricktop's. But the comparisons persisted.

In retrospect, Bricktop would not feel kindly toward West 52nd Street. "In 1957," she later recalled, "Thelma Carpenter, the singer, drove me up and down 52nd Street so I could thumb my nose at all the places from which I'd been fired."[17] In contrast, by the time Bricktop left New York, West 52nd Street had welcomed Mabel Mercer, and at Tony's she at last found a home.

TONY'S

TONY'S WEST SIDE was an intimate rendezvous that catered to the smarter set from Broadway, the East Side contingent, and a sprinkling of world travelers. Originally located on the East Side, it had moved to 59 West 52nd Street in 1929 and, like "21" and others, had survived the transition from speakeasy to legitimate cabaret. In the middle to late Thirties, it attracted primarily struggling artists, actors, and writers who appreciated its lack of cover charge or minimum, and who remained loyal patrons after they became well-to-do and famous. A large mural boasted a group of the club's better-known patrons—actors Pat O'Brien, Lily Pons, Osgood Perkins (father of Anthony Perkins), Clark Gable, Roland Young, Katharine Hepburn, and Charles Laughton; columnist Walter Winchell; Harold Ross, editor of *The New Yorker*; singer Marlene Dietrich, dancer Fred

Astaire, impresario Dwight Wiman, and British comedy star Beatrice Lillie. Julie, the hat check girl, knew most of the patrons by name; Louis, the bartender, stood ready to serve any kind of drink, from Napoleon brandy to a Singapore Sling; Spivy, who accompanied herself on the piano at the back of the club, enjoyed a devoted following (which she took with her when she left to open Spivy's); and Tony Soma, the host, was known, when the spirit moved him, to sing "*Vesti la guibba*" from *I Pagliacci* while standing on his head.

Tony's was located to the west of Ryan's, a new, down-home jazz place. According to one story, one night after the Metropolitan Opera had begun its season, a man in tails and a girl in a mink climbed out of a cab and entered Ryan's. Ryan himself was standing by the door and he had an idea that the couple had come to the wrong place. The jazz band was blaring, drunks were arguing at the bar, and the smoke was so thick nobody could see the bandstand. Said the girl to her escort, "I told you the West Side would be dreadful."[1]

But West Fifty-second street was not so easily categorized. Says Eddie Jaffe, "West Fifty-second street had a number of different sides to it. One was the raucous comedy of Jackie Gleason and the original insult comedy. It also had the jazz element. Then it had the clip-joint element—clubs where there were girls whose job it was to get people to buy drinks. Each place was different, and the combination didn't mix. Tony's, I remember, was a very dignified place."

By 1942, Tony's had become the place where one could enjoy East Side on the West Side. With the desertion of Spivy, Tony Soma had opted for a more refined but no less loyalty-inspiring type of entertainment. Cy Walter, and then Mabel Mercer, suited this style. It was romantic, it touched the soul, and in wartime there were patrons in abundance who wanted just that kind of atmosphere and were willing to pay for it.

Even before the United States had officially entered the war, there had been a boom in the New York nightclub business. With most of the cities of Europe blacked out, New York had become the world center for night life. Wrote Jane Cobb in *The New York Times* in 1941, "New York is a good nightclub city for a variety of reasons. Population counts, of course, and then there are the transients—salesmen and sightseers count. But the principal reason why New York—in America, at least—is the promised land of all cafe society addicts seems to lie in the fact that it contains so many people whose well-being—both psychic and financial—depends on their being seen in the Right Places. . . . Why they should wish to do this night after night at no little expense is simply a problem in human psychology; but a really fashionable nightclub has a fascination that even the most belligerent social conscience finds hard to resist. There is a comfortable I-have-been-here-before feeling that makes every New Yorker realize how lucky he is."[2]

America's entry into the war provided still another boon for the New York nightclub business: on any given night, some twenty percent of the patrons of the clubs were servicemen, whose money, if not their cachet, was as good as anyone else's. Not a few who became diehard Mabel Mercer fans heard her first when they were soldiers or sailors on leave in New York, and many of them were introduced by buddies who had already come under Mabel's spell. Bart Howard was among them. Before he was shipped overseas, he regularly went to New York on furlough to hear Mabel.

"I was really lucky. I was in Georgia for three years, an infantry instructor and all, but no doubt they kept me because I played the piano. Eventually, they had to send me out, so they sent me out with a hospital unit to England, and I spent the rest of my war in England. I remember I sent Mabel a score to a Noel Coward show, and when I came back she was singing the songs. We corresponded; I wish I had saved those letters, but in the army it's hard to save things."

At Tony's, Mabel was able to recreate the magic that she had first developed at Bricktop's. Her voice may have changed, but her way with a lyric had not. In the small club with its tiny stage, she moved easily from table to table, but as the years passed she learned that she could be just as effective simply sitting in a chair next to the piano. She sat with her hands folded in her lap, using them only sparingly to express a line more profoundly. She sang the songs that the patrons of the club wanted to hear, and she sang them in a way that caused them to believe she was singing those songs just for them.

Allen Carter, who first saw Mabel at Tony's in 1945, recalls that Mabel usually mounted the small stage around eleven o'clock: "Before eleven o'clock Tony had tables all over—even in the back there was a table area at the bar, and up front there were tables and there was a platform with the piano, and for dinner there would be tables all around the piano. Come eleven o'clock, or after the dinner crowd left, the tables would be removed from the platform and Mabel's chair would go up on the platform in front of the piano. Mabel would come out and start to sing—and don't let anyone talk while she was singing because she'd stop right in the middle of a song. And then of course whoever was talking would realize it and would stop and Mabel would continue. The number of songs she sang depended on her mood and how many people were there. A lot of times— she did this several times when I was in there alone—she sat at the table with me and sang from the table. She would sing, oh maybe four, five, six songs, whatever, and then she'd stop, and whenever the mood struck her, or if people left and new people came in, she would sing again. She was there every night until four A.M."

Tony Soma never demanded that she sing a certain number of songs or a certain number of minutes; he let her sing what she felt like when she felt like singing it. And if she had a late theater date, he did not mind if she arrived after eleven o'clock. Nor did his patrons seem to mind if she sang three songs or four, or whether she started singing at eleven o'clock or at eleven-thirty. But when she did sing, they liked it, and what she did sing, they loved.

She "fit" at Tony's, and after the first six months or so had passed and Tony did not ask her to leave, she began to hope that she had found a place where she could belong, where she could settle in. Once she started to feel secure at Tony's, she began to put down some home roots as well.

In the 1943–44 *New York Telephone Directory*, Mabel listed herself for the first time—45 West 110th Street, UN4-4984. Kelsey Pharr was listed at that address and telephone number as well, but since he was rarely in town Mabel felt that it was essentially her apartment. She acquired a piano for the living room, stocked the kitchen with staples—including a cabinet full of nonperishable items for emergencies, evidence of her childhood deprivation and her later experience of wartime shortages—and in no time at all had welcomed several stray cats and dogs.

"It was a two-bedroom apartment," Allen Carter recalls. "It had a very large living room facing the park; the dining room was large also. I never saw the bedrooms. It was an old building that was kept up—that whole street was kept up." The wide boulevard that would later be called Central Park North was at the north end of Central Park, the 600-acre rectangle of greenery in Manhattan that was Mabel's favorite part of the city. Even though she had a view of the park, she immediately planted flowers in her window boxes. It was a fashionable building, with a night doorman and a day doorman, and the neighborhood was genteel and replete with cabs that would take her to Tony's in the evening and return her to her home in the wee hours of the morning, on the rare mornings when she did not have an escort.

Mabel had no shortage of escorts. She had a way of making fast friendships with a great assortment of people who, having become enamored of her performances, quickly also became enamored of her. While these friends included both men and women, she preferred the men as escorts to shows and parties, or even dinner in a restaurant, and there were any number who were willing to oblige.

Allen Carter was among them. "My introduction to her was through Button Taylor—her real name was Sheila—one of the Taylors of Newport. Button and I saw an awful lot of each other in those years. Button and I went to Tony's and she introduced me to Mabel, and from then on Mabel and I were very, very close friends. I would pick Mabel up or she would meet me at the theater for a Saturday matinee and we would go to the theater and then we'd go to Sardi's afterward. Or we'd go to the theater and I'd meet her for dinner. She had an awful lot of leeway at Tony's, and we could go to the theater in the evening and it made no difference what time she showed up at Tony's, because Tony was Tony and as long as she showed up he really didn't care.

"Normally, if Mabel didn't have a theater date or something, she would show up at Tony's around eleven o'clock, and she would sing, off and on, until four o'clock. More than once I closed up Tony's at four A.M. with Mabel and we would get a taxi and go over to Longchamps on Madison Avenue and have a bite to eat and maybe some ice cream. Then I would see Mabel home.

"One of the first times I said to her, 'Let's have dinner and go to the theater,' she said, 'Fine, when?' I named a show that neither of us had seen, and then I said, 'Where would you like to have dinner?' She said, 'I don't know, where would you like to go?' I said, 'Let's go to "21," ' and Mabel didn't hem and haw. She said, 'Hold on, there, let's not get too rambunctious. Let's go to Tony's or Sardi's for dinner. No "21." ' I said, 'Fine, if that's what you want.' And then a few days later I mentioned this to someone and they said, 'Don't you know that "21" won't admit any blacks?' I was not aware of this. I did not go back to '21' for a number of years—it just galled me that they would not let someone of Mabel's stature in, no matter what her color."

The vast majority of the people Mabel met through Tony's were white; indeed, she moved in an almost exclusively white world. But she never forgot who she was. She did not emphasize her color, but she knew what lines she could not cross—and she chose not to try to cross them. Her black friends understood, and in fact none of them ever felt strange on West 52nd Street.

In August 1944, actress Rosetta LeNoire opened on Broadway in director Abram Hill's American Negro Theater adaptation of Philip Yordan's *Anna Lucasta*, which ran for 900 performances, becoming one of Broadway's longest-running musical plays. "I remember coming out of theaters where I was working and going straight to 52nd Street with Frank Silvera, Sidney Poitier, Harry Belafonte, and a bunch of people. We didn't know which of those brownstones we were going into, and we'd end up going from one brownstone to the other until somebody said, 'Hey, we've got a matinee tomorrow, we better get home and get some sleep.' Everybody did it, white and black. We'd meet each other all the time.

"Mabel and I, being Catholic, would also see each other at church. There were many, many holy days that we were downtown working. She'd say, 'Rosie, I saw you at St. Patrick's,' because no matter where we were working we were at St. Patrick's on holy days. Other times, we'd go to St. Malachi's, the actor's chapel. Father Peter O'Brien was good to all the women in the theater. He became Mary Lou Williams's manager."

The warmth and friendliness of 52nd Street was only enhanced by the presence of Mabel, who had a way of making everyone feel as if they belonged. John A. Morton, Jr., one of her listeners at "Theatrical Tony's," as he calls the club, remembers that her "affectionate listeners" included Lena Horne, Ethel Merman, Hazel Webster, Irene Castle, Tallulah Bankhead, Estelle Winwood, Paula Lawrence, Edith Atwater, Hope Williams, Nancy Walker, Charles Butterworth, John Kriza, John Taras, Harry Belafonte, Clifton Webb, Burgess Meredith, Franchot Tone, Jimmy Donohue, Monty Woolley, and Robert Benchley.[3]

Recalls artist Beata Gray, "At Tony's, people would come barreling in, and greet her with open arms, and Mabel would greet them with open arms. And then she'd turn to me if I was sitting there and whisper, 'Who is that?' But she acted that way with everybody, and everybody who went to hear her sing always felt—this was one of her great attributes—as though she was singing directly at them. And she always remembered the songs that people particularly loved. They thought, 'Mabel is singing just to me tonight.' ''

Gray first heard Mabel when she went to Tony's to meet a friend who had been a fan of Mabel's since hearing her in the Bahamas around 1940. "My friend said to me, 'Beata, you will find out that there isn't a song you will hear on the stage that Mabel will not have destroyed for you.' And that was true, because after I'd heard her singing 'Come Rain or Come Shine'—I think it was from *St. Louis Woman* on the stage—the song with a backup and an orchestra and the sets and everything else just didn't come across the way Mabel did it just sitting by the piano and singing. I remember very distinctly that that first night I walked into Tony's, she was singing 'September Song.' ''

That night was also the first time Gray had ever walked into a nightclub alone, but after she met Mabel she never again felt odd entering a club by herself where Mabel was singing. "She was so sweet. She would always seat me at a table with someone else, so I wouldn't be alone."

Yet another female artist who became friendly with Mabel while she was at Tony's was Lisa Rhana, one of the youngest artists ever to have done covers for *The New Yorker, Time, Dance, Theatre, Vanity Fair,* and London *Vogue.* Mabel sat for a pastel portrait by Rhana in 1946 and thereafter it hung on the wall at Tony's. One evening a fire broke out at the club, but a quick-thinking waiter rescued the portrait. It was always Mabel's favorite.

As the years passed at Tony's, Mabel developed a devoted following among people like Allen Carter and Beata Gray and retained the allegiance of those who had known her in Paris at Bricktop's. "Mabel knew everybody who was anybody," says Carter. "The Duke and Duchess of Windsor, when they were in New York, would go to Tony's and sit for hours and listen to Mabel. Millicent Rogers, whom I knew quite well, was very fond of Mabel. I was in Tony's one night by myself sitting at a table, and Mabel and I were talking, and Millicent's name came up. I said, 'You know Millicent?' and she said, 'Yes,' and I said, 'I think I'll go call her and ask her to come by.' She said, 'You're not going to,' and I said, 'Of course I am.' But Millicent didn't want to get up at twelve o'clock and come out, even to see Mabel.''

There were the Taylors of Newport and Cordelia Biddle Robinson and Doris Duke, and of course Joe Carstairs. There were also the less well-known people. Mabel treated them all the same, and helped those who needed help whenever she could. At the time, Allen Carter was a young, struggling actor who lived primarily on the allowance he received from his parents. "One time my father inadvertently put an extra initial in my name when he wrote out the check to me. And at that time in New York it was a bitch to try and cash a check, even in a bank where I was known. I took this check into Manufacturers Hanover, my bank, and they wouldn't cash it. In desperation, I called Mabel at home and said, 'I have a check and the bank won't cash it for me. I know Tony will cash it for me.' She said, 'Of course, come up.' I got into a cab, and I had the cab wait, and she gave me the money I needed, and I said, 'I'll see you at Tony's tonight,' and I did. She never asked me for the money. I handed it to her, and my first question was, 'Did Tony cash it for you?' and she said, 'Of course.' Now whether it took her short that day or not was immaterial.''

In return for the kindnesses Mabel did for them, her friends tried to help her whenever they could. More often than not, for people like Allen Carter, doing something nice for Mabel meant taking her to dinner and a show, or cheering her up when she felt depressed—or at least intending to. Says Carter, "On a Sunday afternoon if she were feeling low and blue she'd call and ask, 'Do you feel like going to a movie?' I'd say yes and we'd go to a movie and then have a bite to eat afterward. The movie would cheer her up, and I'd cry on her shoulder and she'd listen to me and never tell me why she was blue." Carter suspected that one reason might be her failure to reach real stardom, and on one occasion in the early years of their friendship Carter attempted to help get her on Broadway.

"She always wanted to do a real Broadway show—always," says Carter, whose shared love for the theater was one of the things that helped cement his relationship with Mabel. While Mabel liked the security of Tony's, she had learned long ago that nothing lasts forever, and in quiet moments she sometimes feared what would become of her. She was in her midforties and still lacked the stability of a solid bank account. She worried, too, that the vagaries of fortune had conspired to keep her career at a relatively low rung. While most of the time she professed to be glad that she had no head for business matters, she realized that she simply hadn't the aggressiveness in her to become a big star, and on occasion she dreamed of the very stardom she was unwilling or unable to go after.

She felt particular conflict when word got around that Jerome Kern and others were planning a revival of *Show Boat* on Broadway. Mabel had a special place in her heart for that show ever since she had appeared in the London production starring Paul Robeson in the 1920s. Back then, she had dreamed of playing the part of Julie, the "quadroon," and that dream had stayed with her, although she was far too reticent to mention it.

Allen Carter, however, knew that she would like to appear on Broadway, and when he learned of the plans for a revival of *Show Boat*, he immediately thought of Mabel. "I knew one of the producers, and I said to Mabel, 'You know, you would be great as Julie.' She said, 'I don't know. They'll probably prefer someone to "darken up" for that [that is, to get a white actress to play the role in dark makeup].' I said, 'Let me mention it and see what happens.' I did mention it, but I never told Mabel what was said. Number one, she was too old at the time to do Julie. And number two, it was Lena Horne's story."

Jerome Kern had specifically asked that Lena Horne play the role of Julie, and Lena was eager to do so. In fact, if she had not been involved in a power struggle with Metro-Goldwyn-Mayer, it would indeed have been "her story." Arthur Freed, who had solid connections with M-G-M, had wanted Lena for the title role in the play *St. Louis Woman*, and the studio had agreed to allow her to take the role. But Lena refused because she felt the script contained the same old stereotypical black sporting-life roles. Thus, when Kern and company approached M-G-M about her playing Julie in the revival of *Show Boat*, the studio refused to allow her to do it. In the end, just as Mabel had predicted, Ava Gardner got the role, and was "darkened up" with Max Factor's "Light Egyptian" pancake makeup.

"Mabel would have been wonderful in the role," says Rosetta LeNoire, who herself has played the role of Queenie in *Show Boat* "many times, with many, many stars." But Mabel was not destined to be in *Show Boat* on Broadway, nor in any other show. In fact, the only part of Mabel that ever got to Broadway was her voice.

On March 15, 1950, at the Ethel Barrymore Theater, Gian-Carlo Menotti's music drama *The Consul*, based on his Pulitzer Prize-winning opera of the same title, opened starring Patricia Neway and Marie Powers. The highly political story is about the postwar world in which people are becoming displaced in their own countries because the government has ceased to serve them. William Hawkins of the *New York World Telegram* described the opening scene: "The country of the setting is never identified, but its flavor is continental Europe, and its native language, for purposes of projection, is English. At the rise of the first curtain there is the sound of a phonograph record off stage, on which a woman's voice is singing a popular street song. Here is a sharp imitation of one of those insidious, cheap, self-pitying, guttersnipe melodies, at which no one can top the French. It is decadent, cloying and contagious. As sung by Mabel Mercer, it captures the sirenish resignation that makes the song so loathsome to Magda Sorel, the play's chief character."[4]

The song, which Menotti titled "*Tu reviendras*," was interrupted in the performance, and Mabel wanted very much for the composer to complete it so she could add it to her repertoire.

So did a number of other singers. But Menotti refused, explaining that he did not want it sung by other singers or in other places. Mabel had to be content with the knowledge that wherever *The Consul* was performed, her voice was part of it.

At another time, Mabel's rendition of the song, revealing as it did her skills as an actress, might have led to other acting opportunities for her. After all, Mabel Mercer was about as far from a sirenish guttersnipe as one could be. But as Rosetta LeNoire points out, "You have to remember that at that time we were only playing maid's roles. I even had to satisfy myself by going to school and paying money I could ill afford in order to play other roles in class."

Despite her inability to get to Broadway, Mabel enjoyed a modicum of fame as a singer. She was always an "acquired taste" and "for the select few," but the select few were impressive names—or at least many of them were. And they included a number of composers.

One was Larry Hart. "He was a little man—short, I mean," Mabel recalled in a 1982 National Public Radio program. "He seemed to be rather a lonely man, I thought, because he used to come into the club quite often and sit and listen to songs. And when he'd hear one of his own songs, he'd be so surprised. He'd say, 'Where did you get that from?' I used to sing 'Little Girl Blue' a lot, and he rushed to me one time and said, 'Tell me, tell me. Where'd you find that?' Well, it was in some show. I wasn't here at the time, I wasn't in America. It always seemed to amaze him that one would be singing his lyrics. He was a very sensitive little man."[5] Another of Hart's songs that Mabel sang often at that time was "Falling in Love With Love."

Says Beata Gray, "Sometimes a song would be thrown out of a show, and she would get it, and make it come alive and become a classic. She also got the lead sheets of musicals before they were produced, and so she would start singing some of the songs even before they appeared on the Broadway stage. I think people just gave them to her."

Allen Carter agrees. "Whenever there was a song to be

introduced, the songwriters would bring it to Mabel. She sang 'Symphony' like no other person in the world. And then of course there was 'My Funny Valentine' by Rodgers and Hart and 'Here I Sit in My Rocking Chair' and 'When in Rome, Do As the Romans Do.' There were so many."

Perhaps Mabel's biggest composer-fan was Alec Wilder, who once said, "There was nothing outstanding about Tony's except Mabel. She made it into a kind of chapel. She gave it an aura of calm and protection. She had magic. People would come in, not just to hear her sing, but to absorb the atmosphere she created—one of great calm and peace and security. Hers was the oddball place. It didn't swing, as some other Fifty-second Street joints did. She didn't attempt to swing.

"She did dozens of songs that I and others felt impelled to write for her, songs that nobody has since heard. They remain in manuscript. And if they did get published, they seem to get lost on some dusty shelf. Like 'The Olive Tree,' published by G. Schirmer, on which I have never received a cent of royalty.

"But she also did songs that became standards because she did them. 'Wait Till You See Her' was a ballad that was not used in *By Jupiter*. But Mabel liked it. After she began singing it, the magical thing happened. Other singers discovered it. Suddenly, the rejected song became a talked-about song. Peggy Lee added it to her repertoire. So did Sinatra. Bandleaders began putting it into their books. Single-handed, Mabel revived other forgotten songs and popularized songs that would have been forgotten. Mabel was the first to see merit in 'While We're Young,' one of my songs and one of the first she did when she began working at Tony's."[6]

Mabel had been interested in Wilder's work ever since she had heard his octets in the Bahamas, and it was not long after her return to New York that the two had gotten to know each other. Wilder, who liked to call himself "president of the 'derrière-garde,'" was a shy, even timid man with whose personality and songs Mabel felt an immediate kinship. Like

Mabel, Wilder believed that in a song the lyric was all, and Wilder's melodic lines always paid tribute to his lyrics, indeed were often written to fit lyrics. Like Mabel, he preferred sad songs, although he always felt that she showed more courage in singing them than he did in writing them. Also like Mabel, he was a very private person, even though he had chosen to present himself as an eccentric in order to shield himself from prying questions, finding that once he was thus categorized he was generally left alone.

Unlike Mabel, he had no need for roots and a home base. Born in Rochester, New York, son of a banker, he had spent most of his childhood years in New York City, where his mother moved after his father's death when Alec was three, and Garden City, Long Island. While attending private schools, he had somehow developed an interest in music, which shocked his mother, who regarded musicians on the level of servants. Alec did not share his mother's attitude toward either musicians or servants, and one summer played piano and banjo in an otherwise all-black dance band at a hotel dance in Bay Head, Long Island. In 1920, he attended performances of Noble Sissle and Eubie Blake's *Shuffle Along* at the Sixty-third Street Theater before the carriage trade discovered the show, and regarded the show as "a revelation" with the same impact as Debussy's *Afternoon of a Faun*.

When he decided to devote himself to writing music, his mother resigned herself to this fact, welcoming him back home whenever he chose to return. The home he himself established was a room at the Algonquin Hotel, which he had first visited as a child and whose staff still included people who remembered him from that time. Yet even after he had lived in that room for years, it contained few vestiges of Alec Wilder. He liked to say that his possessions were limited to three suitcases, and indeed he often traveled. Occasionally, he simply boarded a train and rode as far as it went. Mabel's friend Will Craik, who got to know Wilder in the late 1950s, recalls, "He would wear the same suit until it dropped off, then he'd go out and buy another one. He just didn't care about possessions, which was just the opposite of Mabel. When he'd visit her, he'd say, 'Mabel has got so much stuff around here, I don't see how she can stand it. I live in such a manner I could pack a suitcase and be gone in ten minutes and no one would ever know I existed.' But he did love Mabel and he wrote many of his songs for her."

Among them, in the latter part of the 1940s, was "Did You Ever Cross Over to Sneden's?" which refers to Sneden's Landing in upstate New York, a place where Mabel liked to go on weekends. There were many others. He wrote them on napkins, scraps of paper, whatever was at hand. In 1981, Mabel recalled that while sitting in Tony's one night, he remarked, "It's smoky in here," and promptly wrote a song of that title on the back of an envelope. Some thirty-five years later, she still had the envelope somewhere. Like Cole Porter, Wilder was very particular about the way his songs were sung and insisted that they be sung only as written. Thus, for him to write a song especially for a singer meant that he trusted that singer implicitly, and as far as is known, Mabel never betrayed that trust.

Not just the friendship between Mabel and Wilder, but the whole aura of West 52nd Street in those days seemed to epitomize trust, both personal and professional. According to Wilder, "The Street was like a block party. The area between Fifth and Sixth avenues was total friendship. You felt safe, secure and protected. Everyone seemed to get along with everybody. You talked to anybody and they talked with you. For me, it was a strange experience because crowds generally make me tense. I want to run, to get out. But not 52nd St. It was a great big friendly world. It has never happened since. And I don't think it ever will again. There is little trust today among adults. 52nd St. was a trusting community. It was good for Mabel. She flourished."[7]

On West 52nd Street, Mabel had indeed found a home, not like Paris but similar in the sense of security she got from it. She also had a sense of security from at least being in the same state as her mother was and knowing that she could pick up a telephone and call her. Sometime in the middle to late 1940s, it became possible for Mabel even to visit her mother on occasion.

By then, Mabel's mother was living alone in Williamstown, New York. She lived there in a small cottage and on land that were both reminiscent of the family home in Wales. Whether she had separated from her American husband or whether he had died is not known. She still had to be careful that the neighbors did not get a close look at Mabel when she visited, but at least Mabel could now visit, and she did so with as much regularity as she could, given the distance and her responsibilities at Tony's, which, as the war's end approached, was busier than ever.

Soldiers and sailors returning from Europe flocked to New York's clubs, and those who had remained at home had much to celebrate. Tony's was packed every night. Bart Howard was discharged from the army after nearly five years, and returned to New York, and civilian life, with some trepidation: "I thought, Jesus, I'm thirty years old and it was kind of rough before the war. At least the army looked after me. But, by God, I had a job in two weeks at Spivy's—fifty dollars a week, and she put me right to work." Naturally, he went to see Mabel, and spent as much time as he could at Tony's when he was not working.

Mabel's accompanist at that time was an excellent pianist named Leslie Crosley. Peter Conway, who met Mabel in the late Forties, recalls that Crosley suffered from a nervous condition, among other problems. "By the time I met him, he was a wreck, from alcohol and nerves and a lot of other things. He was a chain smoker, and I was told by people who had been around him that he had been a wreck for a long time. And that was why—wonderful pianist, wonderful accompanist that he was—Mabel had to get rid of him."

Allen Carter recalls, "He ended up in a sanitarium. Tony

paid all his medical expenses. I was in California when he got out, and I ran into him out there at the Cafe Gala where he had come to see Bobby Short. We talked and he related the whole story to me."

Meanwhile, Mabel needed another accompanist. She called Bart Howard, who had been playing at Spivy's for about six months. He remembers, "She said, 'Look, I need to have a pianist. I'll give you twice the money.' I just left Spivy flat, and worked for Mabel for four years. And that's when I began to write songs for Mabel.

"Working with Mabel, I began to realize that she had a real flair for comedy, but she had no songs to do that were like that. In the meantime, I hadn't been able to find a good lyricist and I had started writing my own lyrics. Pretty soon, everything I wrote, Mabel had to hear. She began singing all sorts of my songs, but I started writing songs that were light and gay because she could camp them in a way that her audience, which at Tony's was a very mixed bag—from newspapermen to decorators to dykes to God knows what else—really loved."

Howard and Mabel recorded a couple of songs together during that period. "One was 'You Are Too Beautiful' backed by 'Just One of Those Things.' Then we did 'I Loves You Porgy' and on the back was 'The Twelve Days of Christmas.' That was a twelve-inch record that we did at Mary somebody's studio in 1946. They weren't widely released."

The two grew exceptionally close. "She was like my mother," says Howard. At length, they began to talk about buying a place in the country, and naturally they needed a car. "There was a guy who used to come into the club who was crazy about Mabel's work; he was from Philadelphia and his name was Harry Beard. Well, Harry Beard elected himself to find us a car, and he bought us an old LaSalle, which he brought up from Philadelphia or something, for $750. Mabel and I managed to pay for that, and I garaged it in my neighborhood for $50 a month. I had found myself a friend with whom I lived down on Twenty-eighth Street. It was a cold-water flat and it was $19 a month—and the garage cost $50! Mabel was living on 110th Street, and every night I drove up to 110th Street, picked up Mabel, took her to work, took her back to 110th Street, and then all the f——ing way down to Twenty-eighth Street and put the car in the garage and fell into bed at five-thirty or something. This went on all the time.

"We owned the car for quite a while, and we used to take trips a lot. We went out to the country and we found a place out there—a chicken coop or something. We were going to buy it, but fortunately we didn't.

"We decided on one of our vacations, my friend Bud and I and Mabel, to take the car to Miami and then Joe [Carstairs] would come and pick us up in her boat. So we started out, and we were in south Delaware when the car begins steaming and making all sorts of noises. We are now in that land, the South, and we've got Mabel in the car and we're going to have to find a hotel. Bud and I are in our army khakis, all washed out, and we are both young and blond; Mabel is wearing a scarf over her head. There is nothing for us to do but walk into town. So the three of us walk down the highway and we get to a town and I see a hotel and I see a Japanese man and his wife coming out, and I say, 'We're going in *there*' (because I figure it's already been integrated). There was no trouble about that. We got somebody to get the car from the highway and bring it in.

"That night, Mabel has to do 'some shopping, dear'; she has to go to the drugstore. We got to the drugstore and the man said, 'Oh, are you the two we saw on the road today? I said to myself, there are two GI's and their mother, and I shoulda stopped and picked them up.' Well, from then on, Mabel was our mother!

"So we called Harry Beard. Harry came with his sister, Pearl, who owned a television station in Pennsylvania, and picked us up and drove us to Miami. Very big of him. Joe picked us up in the boat and we spent a month in the Bahamas and then came back to New York. And guess who had to go back down to Delaware and get the car? It cost me another three hundred dollars."

Not many months afterward, in Howard's recollection, Mabel and Tony had a falling out, or as he puts it, "a blowup": "It was New Year's Eve, and it was over ten dollars—she quit because he wasn't going to give her another ten dollars. He kept me on because I didn't have a job, but I was only there about two weeks. I sat there and told people what happened, and that let me out, too."

In Mabel Mercer legend, she left Tony's only because the place was torn down, and the two events did occur around the same time in 1949. But both Mabel and Tony himself left the building before the wrecking ball began to strike. He moved over to the East Side and opened a restaurant called Tony's Wife's Place (some legal difficulty precluded his taking the name of his club with him). Mabel also moved over to the East Side, taking her Lisa Rhana portrait with her to the Byline Room of the East Side Show Spot at 137 East 52nd Street. West 52nd Street was by now in its twilight, the victim both of its own excesses and of progress. The New York State Liquor Authority had started clamping down on the strip joints that had moved in where more legitimate clubs had vacated. A new Esso building had gone up; then the National City Bank had opened a branch next door; on the boards was an office building development and the CBS building, which would occupy the old site of Tony's. Today, the only reminder of the block's show business past are the street signs that proclaim it "Swing Street."

In a way, it was the end of an era, and it might have occurred to Mabel that it was time for her, too, to move on. The war was over, and people who loved Europe were talking about returning there, hoping to find the Paris and the London of the prewar years. Bricktop was among them. Successful as she had been in Mexico City, she longed to return to Paris and recreate her old club. In 1950, she did.

But Bricktop found postwar Paris much changed. "Montmartre looked like a wreck. It hadn't looked all that great by daylight even in the Twenties, but now it wasn't just shabby, it was almost slummy. . . . At night the atmosphere didn't get much better. The places on the Rue Pigalle and Rue Fontaine closed up either at midnight or at one A.M. That was sad. In my day, things were just getting started at that time."[8] Even more disturbing were the anti-American and anti-black prejudice that Bricktop found, and the bureaucratic red tape she had to wade through in order to open a club. When she opened in May 1950, however, and many of her former patrons came, she believed all the trouble had been worth going through. But there were not enough of the old crowd to keep the place going, and after about six months Bricktop concluded, "We were fooling ourselves, trying to recreate the old Paris days. It was like putting Humpty Dumpty together again. Oh, there were some nights, like the opening of Bricktop's, when the place was jammed with people who knew one another. There weren't enough of those nights to keep Bricktop's alive, though."[9] In December, Bricktop moved on to Rome, where she ran successful clubs on the Via Veneto for the next fifteen years.

Back in New York in 1949, when she was making her plans to return to Paris, Bricktop no doubt approached Mabel with the idea of going with her. But Mabel had no wish to return. She tried not even to think about Paris, and would not sing "The Last Time I Saw Paris," even if the song was specially requested. She'd tried singing it once, and as she later told Whitney Balliett, ". . . so many things started going through the back of my mind about Brick's and my little apartment in Paris and so forth that I had to stop and excuse myself."[10] Her motto was "Never look back," and she had no desire to start all over yet again. It was hard enough to have left Tony's—as she once said, "I prefer to stay in one place. It's the only way people know where to find you."[11] She had made friends in New York and elsewhere in the United States, and had carved out her own niche. Her mother was in the States, and she did not wish to be an ocean away from her again. By this time, too, she did not wish to be an ocean away from Harry Beard.

Harry Beard had become more than a fan, and more than a friend on whom she could call when her car broke down in south Delaware. A restaurant manager in Philadelphia, he was a handsome, dapper man (Bart Howard recalls that he wore a diamond pinky ring) with an air of gallantry and intellectualism that Mabel found attractive. And Harry was enamored of Mabel, or at least of the aura around Mabel. That Harry was white and Jewish and Mabel half black and Catholic, or that Harry was some ten years younger than Mabel, never seemed to bother them. Once, in Philadelphia, Mabel was asked to go to the rear of a segregated city trolley and gallant Harry insisted on going with her, although in the recollection of Mabel's friend Adelaide Wallin-Beach, "She said it was funny because they didn't want Harry to go back into the black section. So after that they took taxis when they could afford it. She said she never created a scene—that was that."

If anything bothered Mabel about her relationship with Harry, it was that they were not married—her convent upbringing and her staunch Catholicism would have gnawed at her conscience. But circumstances were such that for a long time it was not possible for them to marry. Says Mabel's friend for many years, Will Craik, "They were both already married to different people. Harry was separated from his wife—he left his wife to go with Mabel—and a divorce would have been messy. She was still married to Kelsey Pharr, although that was never anything but a paper marriage. She rarely saw him after she came here to the States, although I believe she spent a little bit of time in Florida with his people. . . . I met Kelsey once. He came in to see her performing one time. He never bothered her, never tried to trade on their relationship, because of course she became much more famous than he.

"They never divorced. And Harry, I don't think, divorced his wife for a long time. So, in the beginning they couldn't get married, or decided it would all be too messy. I think they decided it was best to let sleeping dogs lie."

They were very discreet. Eddie Jaffe remembers that this was Mabel's style anyway: "I don't recall her ever having any relationships at the clubs. I don't even remember who she came or left with." People who considered themselves close friends of Mabel's never realized that Harry and Mabel were lovers. He seemed just one among many, many people who were close to Mabel. Says Bart Howard, "I never knew Mabel to have a love affair with anybody. If she did it, she sure did it on the sly. Her closer life with Harry happened when I was on my own tack and not seeing so much of her, and I was delighted that she had someone like Harry—and his sister, Pearl. Mabel grew up feeling she didn't have a family, and she made a family of the world. That's just about what it was—she made everybody her family."

CHAPTER

V

HER FIFTIES

MABEL turned fifty in 1950, and Bart Howard believed that this was a milestone she would just as soon not have reached. He wrote a song especially for her, and presented it to her as a fiftieth birthday present:

It Was Worth It
(That's What I'll Say)

The first day a woman lies about her age
Is the day she starts to think,
Either starts to think . . . or drink.
The first day a woman finds a wrinkle in her face
Is the first day she gets shocked,
And she either gives up liquor . . . or gets crocked.
But I'm not gonna lie about my years,
Get high and cry in my beers.

What's the use of making things worse?
I'd rather up and sing this little verse.

All in all, it was worth it!
Oh, that's what I'll say
To the ladies the very first day
They discover my first bit of gray.

All in all, it was worth it,
I'll say it again,
Can I curse my past gaieties when
They were all of them men?

Oh, why should I browse thru my wrinkles,
Regretting them?
After all, I sure had a ball
While getting them.

The sag must come—
Why be sad it appears;
At least I have had it,
My dears,
That's what I'll say!

Oh, years go by in mem'ry—
I'll fly with romance again;
When down in the dumps I can
Put on me pumps
And dance
Again,

And who can tell—
With a slight overhaul
I could still be the
Belle of the ball,
That's what I'll say!

"It really worked," says Howard, "because from then on she did it almost every show—and continued to do so until way late, until the early to mid-Sixties, until she started doing other people's comedy and my song wasn't done as much. But she really did it—I mean, this was a song that she did as much as 'It Was Just One of Those Things,' which was her big song. And it really was her, and I thought it was the attitude she should have, because I thought she had a problem being fifty. Years later, I was talking about this in front of her, and she said, 'I had no problem being fifty!' All those years, and I'd been mistaken!"

Mabel had little reason to regret turning fifty—she was working, she had Harry, she had more friends than she could count and more fans than she could ever have imagined. She was still not widely known, and evidence that she would like to have been more widely known is the fact that she kept a clipping from early 1951 in which disc jockey Art Ford called her the "Most Un-Appreciated Genius of Popular Music" and said, "Here's hoping 1951 brings her wider recognition."[1] But she liked what renown she did have, and had quickly settled in at the Byline Room; and although it was not Tony's, it was comfortable for her. One writer described it this way: "The Byline Room, which offers only drinks and Mabel Mercer, is usually packed to the doors. It is by no means one of Manhattan's de-luxe bistros, and the mechanics of the place make it necessary for Mabel to have an arrangement with the Show Spot, so that when Mabel sings above, they turn off the music down below."[2]

Squibs in the "Goings On About Town" section of *The New Yorker* indicate the contrast: While the Byline Room is described as an upstairs salon and a midget inglenook, and Mabel's performances as peaceful at-homes and symposia on the care and feeding of contemporary love life, the Show Spot Bar downstairs is febrile, rampageous, raucous, tumultuous, a Donnybrook Fair, and a Mermaid Tavern.

The character of the downstairs spot notwithstanding, Mabel liked the smallness, at least, of the Byline Room. Says Eddie Jaffe, "I don't think we seated more than fifty people upstairs." If Mabel had any complaints about the shape and organization of the club, she did not voice them, but Jaffe recalls that it wasn't a particularly good room. "It was narrow. The ideal room would have been one where all her fans could be as close to her as was physically possible, rather than some right up on top of her and the rest too far away. I remember that so many celebrities came in to hear her and, you know, in a club you tried to 'dress the room,' to put the celebrities at the best tables. But there wasn't too much of that because the room was so small. They were happy just to get in.

"Her main fans were other singers," continues Jaffe. "You had to be another singer to understand how great she was. I don't think the general public ever really understood her singing."

But there were plenty of non-singers who were Mabel Mercer fans, attracted by the worldliness of her delivery, the suggestion that she had been through just about everything about which the lyrics told, the "stately boredom," as one writer put it; or, on the other hand, the suggestion that she was at that moment going through the stories the lyrics told, the immediacy of the emotions. Mabel was enigmatic, a tabula rasa onto which her listeners projected their own emotions.

On any given night, the Windsors, John Huston (who would marry Tony Soma's daughter Ricky), Jose Ferrer, John Gielgud, Eileen Farrell, Zachary Scott, and other luminaries rubbed elbows with the lesser lights among Mabel aficionados—Beata Gray and Peter Conway and others. Her coterie at the Byline Room also included a whole new generation of young people whose parents had heard her in Paris or who had heard her on the records she had made with some increasing frequency toward the late Forties. These were 12-inch records released by small companies and purchased primarily by those who had fallen under her spell at Tony's or who were adventurous enough to purchase records that were regarded as esoteric. She was a particular favorite among college students, and back when she and Bart Howard were at Tony's they were invited to perform at Hamilton College in upstate New York. While Mabel welcomed the affection of young people, she was concerned that they were spending too much time and money at the Byline Room, and on at least one occasion she called a girl's parents to say, "You have a fine girl who needs looking after. I've sent her home." On another occasion, a young girl was in the club every night for three weeks running and eventually attempted suicide. Mabel made it her business to help the girl, and apparently succeeded in getting her to realize that life was worth living after all.[3]

Peter Conway was at Swarthmore College when he first saw Mabel. "It was 1949, I guess. I went to New York with one of my professors from college. I'd always been interested in hearing this woman. She sang Alec Wilder, and I liked Alec Wilder very much. So we went, and it was fabulous. It was a terribly cold, bitter night, and there couldn't have been more than five or six people, literally, in the Byline Room. Mabel did a show—actually, Mabel never did shows, she just got up and sang. She sang as long as we wanted to hear her until the normal closing time, which was around two-thirty to three. We spent the entire evening there. She came over and talked with us, sat with us, chatted—'Happy you're here. Glad you like Alec Wilder.' There were a number of songs by Bart Howard also."

After graduating from college, Conway enrolled at Yale for graduate work and continued to visit New York, and the Byline Room. He became friends with Mabel and a very good friend of Sam Hamilton, who was Mabel's accompanist by the time she went to the Byline Room. Among Mabel's accompanists, Hamilton was not the best pianist of the lot, but he was one of the most loyal, and one of Mabel's closest friends. Conway does not feel that Mabel gave Hamilton enough credit, either for his piano playing or for his friendship. "She used to bang on the piano with her fist if the tempo was too fast or something. If the tempo did not suit her, she would turn around in her chair, just wheel around suddenly, and bang on the piano and make him slow down or pick up or whatever. She never treated him as an equal—God knows, never as an equal!—but never even nicely as a servant. It was always as if he didn't know as much about music as she did. And yet, he was the one who carried her along so often—kept her on tempo, kept her on pitch. That banging on the piano with her fist was a very good example to me of how little she regarded their 'fifty-fifty' arrangement."

For his part, Sam did have the irritating habit of hovering over Mabel and worrying about her too much. He felt she was too generous toward the young people who seemed to gravitate to her. Peter Conway remembers there was one girl in particular. "Sam was quite scandalized—'Nobody knows what's going on, Mabel is making a fool of herself over this young girl. She's in the club every night and Mabel is just giving her this and giving her that. She's putting her up somewhere. I don't know what's wrong with her. She's lost her mind.' Then this girl just sort of disappeared . . . I don't know where she went, but a lot of people were relieved when she left."

Such events fed the periodic rumors that Mabel was a lesbian. So did the coterie of single women who surrounded her. In 1953, *Park East*, an East Side glossy that was published for about a decade, ran an article about her by Roland Wild in which Wild suggested that Mabel's desire to help young women sprang from "a frustrated maternal complex." Peter Conway, for one, did not feel there was anything offensive in the article, although "It made it quite clear that she was illegitimate, although it didn't actually say so. This was a Fifties story, so things were very different then. It also had a lot to say about her friendships with young women, which did not imply in any way, I felt, that there had been any kind of sexual involvement—just that she was involved with younger girls who perhaps had as hard a time as she had had. But she did not seem to take it that way. Of course she did have a great many lesbian friends. But Mabel was deeply offended. Sam told me that she'd told the guy who'd written it, who'd been a friend of hers up until then, that she would never speak to him again."

According to Allen Carter, rumors that Mabel was a lesbian

dated back to her tenure at Tony's. "Thelma Carpenter was a very, very close friend of hers. Thelma came into Tony's one night, and she came to my table, and she stayed late, and then we all went over to Longchamps. One of the columnists had alluded to the fact that Thelma and Mabel were lovers, and that infuriated them both, because it wasn't true. We talked for an hour or so on that and then we took Thelma home and I dropped Mabel off." There was little Mabel could do about such things—and she certainly did not intend to change the way she treated people because of a few rumors.

What bothered Mabel more than these rumors and more than even turning fifty was being fifty without proper roots. In effect, she was still a woman without a country. That she could do something about, however, and in 1952 she became an American citizen. Joe Carstairs believes that Mabel sought citizenship not so much from national loyalty as from the realistic awareness that as a citizen she would have an easier time getting working papers.

Whatever meaning citizenship held for Mabel, during her fifties she thirsted for a home place as much as she did a homeland. Indeed, she had never had a place that belonged to her alone, a little bit of God's earth where she could create her own version of heaven, where plants could grow and animals could thrive and people could rest from their worldly cares. This was the one thing she needed in a deeply felt, uncommunicable way.

She'd already been looking for a place in the country for several years. Spending time in the country with her mother had reinforced in Mabel her own desire to put down roots—a city apartment, no matter what the view out the window or how many flowers graced the window boxes, in Mabel's view, was not enough. Her mother's place in Williamstown, New York, seemed too far away from Mabel's New York City audience for her to consider settling there. Beata Gray's place in Dover Plains was far more suitable and convenient.

"I lived in the country for a while in the late Forties," says

Gray, "and Mabel used to come up to visit us for weekends. She was simply wonderful. She'd go out and dig and weed the garden and come back all covered in mud. And she'd cook—she was a great cook. She talked about getting a place of her own. And once, when she was visiting, we talked about opening an inn, and we would take turns running it. But nothing ever came of it."

Still, Mabel had had a taste of the country, and by 1947 or 1948 she had begun to dream of buying herself a house in the Berkshires, which folks on the New York side call "upcountry" to distinguish it from upstate on the other side of the Hudson. She began reading the "Farms and Acreage" ads in the Sunday *New York Times*, looking for a property that she could afford and that would not be an impossible commute from the city. When she found something that had promise, she got someone to drive her up for a look. At least that was the case until she and Bart Howard bought their LaSalle, the purchase of which Mabel had urged primarily because it was far more convenient to have a car for country-place looking than not to have one.

It had to be a particular place—not only not too expensive, but also one that "spoke" to Mabel and said "This is home." She looked for years for such a place. In the meantime, she began a program of concentrated saving, so that when she did find something she would be able to pay cash for it—no mortgages for Mabel, she didn't want to have to worry about mortgage payments. When she found her roots, she wanted them bought and paid for.

This was her dream—more than Broadway or stardom. Beata Gray chuckles when she remembers, "You know, before she bought the house in the country, she started collecting things for *when* she had a house in the country. Her apartment was jammed with furniture—extra refrigerators and things. It was unbelievable—*un*believable."

And when Mabel daydreamed, it was about the flowers she would plant and the birds she would feed and the cats and dogs to which she would provide a haven, and the home place to which she would go every weekend.

100

It was sometime in 1951 that she learned about the Briggs place in Red Rock, near Chatham, New York, in the foothills of the Berkshires not far from Lenox, Massachusetts, and went to see it. "She responded to a broker's ad," says the house's former owner Charlie Briggs, retired postman and general store owner in Chatham. "The broker showed her the property, and when she became interested the broker had me go around with her, show her where it was. She came two, three times. She was a very, very gracious lady, very big-hearted, a wonderful person. She had friends with her, she had lots of friends. Didn't bring Mr. Beard with her—I don't think he was her manager at the time."

Mabel later recalled, "I first saw this place on a February day in the early Fifties, and it immediately reminded me of Wales, where I spent summers as a child. There was snow on the ground, and I had on high heels, but I walked across the field and down to the stream and up to the waterfall."[4]

"She just loved the place, the country, that spot," says Briggs. "Took about a month for her to settle on it. She was very busy at the time."

Busy—working and trying to get together the money to buy the place. Mabel still resisted tying her roots to a mortgage, even if she had been able to qualify for one. She was not a wealthy woman, by any means. According to Eddie Jaffe, who was doing publicity for the Show Spot and the Byline Room, "A performer made 'as little as possible' [in the view of management]. The economics of that kind of club were against it. I got twenty-five to fifty dollars a week. She probably got a couple hundred dollars. It was a custom that the performers would get the cover—the cover charge. The club would get the liquor money—there was a two-drink minimum. One way or another, it came down to that. In terms of the value of the dollar, it wasn't bad for her. I think it was more important to her to be in a small room that was suited to her than in a big room even though she might have made more money."

Mabel used most of her savings and may have borrowed against her salary in order to pay cash for the place. She may also have borrowed from her friends. But she came up with the money and had her home place at last, an eighteenth-century farmhouse which Briggs's father had bought in the early years of the twentieth century when Chatham was an important rail center. Cape Cod style, it had a center door flanked by matching windows; an ell had been added to one side at some point. It sat close to the ground at the end of a short driveway that led from a road that hadn't been electrified until about 1947 and still wasn't paved, making it nearly impassable much of the year.

"I was born in there," says Charlie Briggs of the house, "lived there forty-one years. 'Course there wasn't any plumbing or heating in it when we had it. She added that. Added on to it three different times."

That Mabel Mercer was "colored" didn't bother Charlie Briggs, who was more concerned with the humanity than with the color of the person who bought the Briggs homestead and who recognized the goodness in Mabel Mercer. "I had a Downs syndrome brother and Mabel was very fond of him and very kind to him. He was a very gentle, loving person, and she always liked to see him and gave him candy and cookies and always gave him a Christmas present. People in town were upset to a certain extent, but when they realized what kind of person she was, it changed. They didn't realize she was a celebrity. I didn't either."

Red Rock, in "upcountry" New York, may have been only a few hours' drive from Manhattan, but it was a world away. Says Father Lee Smith, an old friend of Mabel's, "At the time, there were very, very few blacks up here. The only ones were the descendants of the indentured servants to the old Dutch patroons—like Hilda and Fannie Van Ness. Fannie still wears high-button black shoes and she still refers to us as the white folk and they still have a summer and a winter kitchen."

A twentieth-century black person was another matter. There was talk, and there were looks. Remembers Will Craik, who eventually moved up to Chatham, too, "She was probably the first black around here that owned a house. Later, Sidney Poitier bought a house over in Kinderhook. . . . I got very annoyed one time. George Wein [jazz producer and originator of the Newport, now Kool, Jazz Festival] and his wife, Joyce, came up one time. He's white and she's black, and they came to my house for a barbecue. They decided to take a walk. The next day I was in the Country Store in Old Chatham, in the coffee shop. I was behind the wall—nobody could see me—and I heard somebody saying, 'Did you see that couple walking by the lake yesterday? She was black and he was white. I wonder who they were visiting.' And I couldn't resist: I leaned around the corner and said, 'They were visiting me.' "

Mabel was aware of the talk, and she tried very hard not to offend. It apparently never occurred to her to announce that she was Mabel Mercer, nightclub singer, recording artist, singer's singer, songwriter's singer, beloved of generations. In fact, no doubt remembering how her bohemian family had been regarded when she was a child, she was loath to let her neighbors know that she was in show business for fear that they would adopt the same disapproving attitude as had her grand-mother's neighbors years before. Will Craik recalls, "She was very sensitive. It wasn't the color issue particularly; it was also her fear that people would talk about 'that theatrical crowd up on the hill.' She wanted everyone who visited her to be so circumspect. There was a very, very hot day in August, and there was a group of us up there and we were going into Chatham to shop. We came downstairs, and we all had shorts on, and Mabel was horrified. She said, 'They may get away with that in New York, but they would never get away with that up here.' And she made us go back upstairs and put on slacks. And of course we got to Chatham and we were the only ones in town without shorts on, so she never brought the issue up again. She was so concerned about being called bohemian. She didn't like what she called outrageous behavior. I know several times somebody may have had a couple of drinks during the day and wanted to go into town with us, and she would not permit that: 'They might smell it on your breath, dear.' She tried very hard to fit into the community and not make a big noise and not get star treatment."

When her neighbor Adde Wallin-Beach rode up on her horse, Mabel's first thought was "Oh, it's started again. They just don't want us around." But Adde was just trying to be friendly. "When I got off the horse and went over and welcomed her, she said she was just so happy to think she was accepted. And I couldn't understand why. We talked about it later, and I said, 'Why wouldn't you be accepted?' But up in Rome or wherever it was up there, with her mother, apparently she wasn't received well at all."

Even though Adde Wallin-Beach became a good friend, Mabel did not talk about her "other life" in the city. Recalls Wallin-Beach, "Not for many years did I know who she was. She never talked about what she did. I knew she was a singer, but I didn't know what kind of singer. Then finally one day I went down to the city—I forget the reason, but my son was in college, at Clemson University, and I met him in the city and we decided to go and see Mabel. Suddenly, we realized that we knew this very famous person and never knew that she *was* this. She never seemed famous to me. She was so unassuming, so down to earth, just like the rest of us. I just thought her singing was beautiful, so different from what I had ever heard. She was the first one to say that she did not have a voice but the way she presented it, her interpretation of a song sounded entirely different from someone else singing the identical song. Famous people were there to hear her, and I was impressed when she introduced me to Duke Ellington, Tony Bennett, and people like that. But she was still Mabel. Even though she was dressed in a beautiful gown and shawl and looked like a gracious queen, she was still the woman I knew in sneakers (because she had trouble with her feet), red socks, dungarees, and sweater, working in her yard."

What was important to Mabel was Adde's attitude years earlier, before she knew who Mabel was. In Adde and Charlie

Briggs, Mabel felt she had two friends, and if others were standoffish at first, they did not act against her. Nobody tried to run her out of town. Later, there would be many other friends, among them Edna St. Vincent Millay and her sister Norma—Mabel became a trustee of Steepletop, the artists' colony that was established at the Millay estate in nearby Austerlitz—and scores of others who enjoyed no renown. Once Mabel started to believe that she would be allowed to have her home place, she began to invest in it all the pent-up dreams and plans she'd had for so many years.

She named the house Blakely, after the convent in which she had been raised. Its acreage was overgrown with weeds, but she destroyed none of them; instead, she painstakingly transplanted the weeds from the areas where she wanted to make flower and vegetable gardens. In singer Ronny Whyte's recollection, she continued to do so: "She would go out and dig and replant the weeds. She had a lot of flowers, but she couldn't tell where the flowers ended and the weeds began. It was just kind of wonderful and wild." She moved all the things she had been saving—the refrigerator, the cabinets—to the house, and worried about such things as electricity and plumbing later. As Joe Carstairs, who visited her not long after she had acquired the property, recalls, "I went up there when it was very, very rough. A whole crowd of us went up, and we took our shower in the stream." The place didn't even have a navigable driveway in the wintertime, but that didn't stop Mabel. She was there every weekend. And to be there every weekend, she learned to drive, although she never succeeded in some of the more refined points of the art. The story goes that early in her driving career, she and Sam Hamilton got into her car after playing at the Byline Room and Mabel prepared to project herself through Central Park to home. "Back up a little, Mabel," said Hamilton. "Don't be silly," Mabel replied, "I haven't learned that yet."5

Each Saturday night, after finishing her last show at the Byline Room, she went to early Mass in Manhattan, then set off for the 127-mile run to Chatham, arriving there early in the morning. "I always intend to sleep when I get there," she once told a reporter for the *Chatham Courier*, "but the view of the Catskills is too lovely, there is my small garden and in the fall, the view is just too beautiful again, so I stay up through the day."[6] She would spend a glorious day and a half, before leaving about six o'clock Monday evening, in order to get back to the city for her first Monday night show. "I often wish there was a forty-eight-hour Sunday," she would say with a sigh.[7] She made the trip in all kinds of weather. In the wintertime, the house was barely accessible—food had to be pulled in on a sled by hand. Mabel would park the car at the bottom of the hill below the house, tie a belt (she called it a "buckle") around her suitcase, and drag it up the incline, a full mile. In the spring, when the thaw came, she had to navigate the road knee-deep in mud. But she was prepared to go through much more in order to get to the one place where she felt whole and complete.

That house and property became Mabel's reason for living. Every spare dime went into improvements. Explained Mabel, "I'd tell whoever was working on the improvements, 'When your bill gets to six hundred dollars, stop work, and when I've paid you, start again.' That way, things never got out of hand."[8]

Around 1953, Mabel had the opportunity to earn a bit of extra money when she recorded three albums for Atlantic—*Songs By Mabel Mercer* Vols. I, II, and III. All were ten-inch, single discs, and for Mabel, this was a major output. While these records gave her the opportunity to reach a wider public, none of them sold especially well. Ahmet and Neshuhi Ertegun, founders of Atlantic Records, however, would eventually get their money's worth, and more, out of those tracks.

One suspects that it was money for the farm that lured Mabel to Chicago for a rare appearance outside New York and her first ever in the Windy City. It was the early summer of 1954, and Mabel agreed to a one-night engagement, "An Eve-

ning With Mabel Mercer," at that city's Blue Angel as a favor
to producer Victor Lownes. Asked for a publicity comment,
Dave Garroway of the *Today* show had this to say: "Writing
an endorsement for Mabel Mercer is kind of like writing a
testimonial for spring water or the Statue of Liberty, except
most people don't know about Mabel, who is as fine as these
two more publicized items. Singers, though, drop into the Show
Spot in New York. There you are sure to see other vocalists
sitting around studying the artist from whom they, along with
Peggy Lee, Frank Sinatra, Jeri Southern, Margaret Whiting, Kay
Starr, Dinah Shore to mention just a few, have learned so much
and have been glad to acknowledge it.

"Mabel is the greatest story-teller in the business today.
The old, old story becomes fresh and alive night after night,
and fires the young part of each old heart. Not to have heard
Mabel sing is to be a little poor in life."[9] Mabel kept that endorsement in her scrapbook, too.

Accompanied by Sam Hamilton, Mabel was a sellout in
Chicago. Wrote Victor Lownes in *Playboy* the following year:
"She packed that night club with over eight hundred turned
away at the door. This, mind you, in a city where she had never
appeared before, on a Sunday, normally the deadest night in
the night club week, and with an admission charge of $5.50.
No funny-hat comics, no chorus line, no party gee-gaws. Just
Mabel. She came as a favor to a friend and left a score of club
owners weeping because she would consider nothing so com-
mercial as an extended return engagement."[10]

The pre-performance publicity announcement had com-
mented wryly, "This engagement should also convince Miss
Mercer that there *really* is a middle west."[11] But the Middle
West did not have Blakely Farm, and that was Mabel's constant
concern. Charlie Briggs looked after the property when she was
away. He cut the field, tapped the trees for maple syrup, and
pulled her out of the ditch a few times. Still, Mabel did not feel
she could impose upon him too much, and she worried about
the place when she was away from it. She was not able to count

on Harry Beard for much help, for he did not share her passion for the farm. In fact, he disapproved of the whole affair, for Mabel at the farm in Red Rock was not the Mabel of nightclubs. She was Mabel in jeans and sneakers and a bandana tied around her head and "earth" under her fingernails, "queen" of a farm that was a warren of little rooms and that they soon dubbed Ramshackle Manor.

It seems likely, therefore, that she not only offered the place to her numerous friends out of friendship, but also with the hope that they would look after it. As far as it is known, only one of them betrayed Mabel's trust, by failing to care for the place properly and by also putting Mabel in an awkward position with her neighbors, the one thing she had tried so hard to avoid. The young woman was the same young woman whom Peter Conway remembered as having caused talk among Mabel's friends and whose attentions from Mabel had so scandalized Sam Hamilton. We will call her Mary.

She came, apparently, from Indianapolis, and she was recently divorced and seemingly vulnerable—just the sort of young woman who brought out the maternal instincts in Mabel. She was also the kind of person who could ingratiate herself so deeply that once she had done so, could hang around one's neck like an albatross. Somehow, she not only got to Red Rock but also spent enough time there to ingratiate herself with the Smilows, neighbors of Mabel's, before prevailing upon Mabel to write to Bricktop in Rome on her behalf, which elicited an invitation from Bricktop to join her in Rome. Bricktop, who was exceptionally generous, and eager to help a friend of Mabel's, not only paid Mary's plane fare to Rome but put her up in her apartment and gave her a job at her Bricktop's on the Via Veneto. But Mary had needed money even before she'd set off for Rome, and had got it from the Smilows.

Fred Smilow was a real estate agent in town, and his wife was an invalid, but Mary managed to get them to cosign a bank loan for her in the spring of 1957. A year later, Mrs. Smilow sent the following letter to Bricktop:

East Chatham, New York
March 31, 1958

Madame Bricktop,
Rome, Italy

Dear Madam:

Our neighbor and friend, Mable [sic] Mercer, tells us that the young lady, ———, will probably not be returning to the USA until late next summer. We have been waiting for her to return, not wanting to trouble others with a personal affair. Now, we feel we must ask you, as a friend and employer, if you will try to persuade her to do the right thing.

After she received your cablegram last spring, she came to us, saying she must have money with which to take belongings to her home in Indianapolis, and pick up a wardrobe there, etc. She claimed that she was expecting a large check daily, from her lawyer. She wanted to borrow the money from the bank in Chatham, to be repaid before she went to Europe. We foolishly endorsed the note. ——— has never paid a cent and of course, we long ago paid the bank. She owes us $400, not counting interest we paid.

We are retired people and can't afford any such loss—which is beside the point anyway. I know, of course, it is no responsibility of yours, but since I understand that you have great influence over this girl, perhaps you will be willing to talk to her about it. We will accept payments in any amount she is able to make, and send her receipts for them.

Please excuse this intrusion of our affairs, but you will understand that with taxes, and other heavy expenses, we have no choice but to do whatever we can to recover this money.

Yours truly,
Mrs. Fred Smilow
East Chatham, N.Y.[12]

Apparently, this was not the only communication from a creditor that Bricktop had received over the past year. Even though Mary had converted to Catholicism in Rome and claimed often that she would never hurt Bricktop either personally or professionally, Bricktop had begun to suspect that she was being had. By the time the letter from Mrs. Smilow had arrived, Mary had moved out of Bricktop's apartment and into a hotel and was sending notes to Bricktop constantly explaining why she could not repay 38,000 lire she owed Bricktop. Among other reasons, she claimed to have hepatitis. Bricktop's papers include a note, in Bricktop's hand, with the name of the bank in Chatham that had extended the loan (information not contained in Mrs. Smilow's letter), so she evidently investigated the matter. Mary apparently told Bricktop that she had sent the money to Mabel, and Bricktop wrote to Mabel to that effect. In May, Mabel wrote to Bricktop:

> New York
> May 16th
>
> Dearest Brick,
>
> I was in the country last Sunday & Mrs. Smilow showed me your letter & I was surprised at ———— saying she had sent me the money. Please do not believe this & thank you for your support. I would hate these people to have any doubt of my honesty. She is a wicked girl & left innumerable debts here & the bills keep coming to my house. I thought being with you would have done her some good especially as she became Catholic. I hope you are well. A friend is kindly bringing you this note & I will write later. I will be working here through June & possibly July.
>
> > Keep well.
> > Much love &
> > again Thank you.
> > Mabel[13]

Apparently, the Smilows did not hold the "Mary" matter against Mabel. Nor did Bricktop, despite many second thoughts, and despite the fact that as late as spring 1961 she was still receiving dunning notices from the United States addressed to the young woman "c/o Brick Top, 155 Via Veneto, Rome, Italy."

On the contrary, Bricktop considered Mabel one of her

closest friends, the ocean between them notwithstanding. Samuel V. K. Willson, who had been a fan of Mabel's since his college days in the late Forties, recalls, "In the late Fifties I stopped in Rome at Bricktop's, and mentioned to the lady that I was a great admirer of Mabel Mercer. That honest remark instantly won me a free drink. I remember King Farouk of Egypt was sitting in the foyer of the bar on a satin chair, like a bored husband waiting for his wife to emerge from the powder room. All evening Bricktop kept asking me about Mabel, but all I could do was tell her what songs she was singing, how many of us Ivy Leaguers adored her, how sensational we thought she was. You'd have thought I was telling Bricktop about a relative, a sister, she was so anxious for news. A few weeks later I was sitting in the square on Capri when I saw Bricktop, all alone, still in Rome clothes, entering the square, surely just off the boat from Naples. *She* recognized *me*, to my immense pleasure: 'You're Mabel's boyfriend, aren't you, sweetheart? Come on, take me to lunch. It's my birthday. I'd rather have lunch on my birthday with a friend of Mabel's than with anybody else in the world.' That's what her *competitors* thought of Mabel Mercer!"[14]

Few of the people Mabel tried to help proved as ungrateful as Mary, and thanks to the acquisition of the farm in Red Rock and a long-term engagement at the Byline room, the mid-Fifties were a happy period for Mabel. At times she wished that her hours at the Byline Room could be as flexible as they had been at Tony's, where nobody minded if she showed up late. At the Byline Room, she was expected to do her first set at eleven, and it was only on rare occasions that she did not meet her commitment. Mabel was serious about her professional responsibilities, and besides, she needed her weekly salary to pay for the house in Red Rock.

Thus, when the East Side Show Spot, and the Byline Room upstairs, burned down in the spring of 1955, it was an anxious time for Mabel. The fire destroyed her second-longest tenure in a club after Tony's. (According to observers of postwar café society, however, she still held the record, with the exception perhaps of Tommy Lyman, of enjoying the longest consecutive record of any solo attraction in New York.) Unfortunately, the famous Lisa Rhana portrait also perished in that fire. The artist would do other pastels of Mabel, but the first was always Mabel's favorite.

While a new Byline Room was under construction on the West Side, Mabel sang at a variety of clubs. One was Jimmy Daniels's Bon Soir in the Village where, according to Rosetta LeNoire, Mabel was always welcome and had only to name the date on which she wanted to perform. Another was the Pin-Up Room, 242 Lexington Avenue at 34th Street, a small, smoky neighborhood bar in the rear of which there was just room for a piano and a singer. Sam Hamilton went with Mabel to the Pin-Up Room where she received rare exposure in the national press when *Newsweek* ran a short article about her in its August 22, 1955, issue. The author of the article wrote, "Today, Mabel Mercer is probably the only singer in the business who would dare face a bleary-eyed night-club audience in the early hours of the morning and sing them a musical setting of A. E. Houseman's poems."[15] Sam Hamilton was pictured with Mabel in the accompanying photograph but was not mentioned in the article. Around the time it appeared, Hamilton left Mabel and New York.

Says Peter Conway, who was a friend of both Sam's and Mabel's, "He felt he was getting nowhere and that Mabel was not treating him right and that he was getting no glory whatsoever. I think he was beginning to feel a little left out. He went into the sporting goods business with a couple of friends in New Canaan, Connecticut. He had visited them there and liked the area, and he moved out of New York bag and baggage—gave up his apartment and everything else. I remember thinking he was giving up a magnificent apartment—a garden apartment in a beautiful old townhouse on East 86th Street off Fifth Avenue, right near the Metropolitan Museum of Art.

"It wasn't such a great adjustment for him really. He was

from Indiana, and what was sort of remarkable about him was that he never lost the Indiana. He was such a sweet, gentle soul—in fact, the last metier you'd think of him in was a night-club or a cabaret. That was what seemed out of key, not New Canaan."

Conway, who had first become friends with Mabel and Sam in 1949 at the old Byline Room, had kept up a frequent correspondence with Hamilton through Conway's years in the army as a theatrical director and entertainer with Army Special Services. Afterward, when Conway set about pursuing a career as a club singer, "Sam was my 'coach,' although he would never call himself that. He was my coach and accompanist at a ridiculously low fee. He played every audition I did, however frequent—sometimes four or five in a single afternoon."

Conway received little help from Mabel. "I don't want to say she was selfish, but I think she was so involved in her own career and its survival that she wasn't very concerned about what other people did unless it directly impinged on her. I wrote a song for her once, that I thought was really quite good, and gave it to her, and she promptly lost it. I asked Sam about it a couple of years later, and he said, 'Oh, you know so many people are giving her material. I never saw it. I don't know if she looked at it or not.' "

Ronnie Selby joined Mabel at the Pin-Up Room, billed as Mabel's "accompanist and interlude pianist," and he went with her when they opened the New Byline Room at 28 West 56th Street (it was formerly a club called the Chi-Chi) in the first week of November 1955. The weather was terrible that night —the rain poured down on Mabel's fans, but they were undeterred. Wrote "Dream Street" columnist Robert Sylvester in the New York *Daily News*, "The room, one of the biggest Mabel has tried, looked like a subway express at the rush hour." As a matter of fact, the club staged no fewer than three opening nights, and considering that "night-owling has just about gone out of fashion," according to *Cue* magazine, that was particularly noteworthy. Of course Mabel had received some important publicity about a month and a half earlier when Walter Winchell had reported in his September 16, 1955, column in the New York *Mirror*, "When Sinatra was at the Composer on 58th [Street] I heard him say: 'Everything I learned I owe to Mabel Mercer.' "[16]

Walter Richie, a fan of Mabel's, may not have the same cachet as Walter Winchell, but Richie's recollections support the columnist's: "I had a brief and insignificant exposure to Sinatra during his period after the initial fame and success and Ava Gardner. He said, 'If you want to see me in New York, I am at the Byline Room on East Fifty-second Street every night. There is a singer there by the name of Mabel Mercer who I think is great. When you see her you'll know why I feel as I do.' Of course, when he made his re-emergence, his new style was a male version of Mabel for phrasing, and he always had the wonderfully clear enunciation that was her trademark."[17]

Barbara Hutton came with her new husband, Baron von Cramm. Mabel's wedding gift to her was a recording of "Strange Interlude," the song Hutton had most often requested of her at Bricktop's in Paris. Mrs. Kumudesh Bhandari, wife of an Indian diplomat, tape-recorded Mabel's songs at the Byline Room and the music at El Morocco as "the sounds which will make her most nostalgic about New York."[18]

Allen Carter, among others, followed Mabel to the New Byline Room and became a regular there. "I remember one evening I was in there. It was a winter evening and there were very few people in the club, and Mabel was very, very late. Eddy Ramshaw, who owned the club with his wife, Mildred, was always sort of hovering around the door, and when she [Mabel] finally came in—I think she had been to a party or something and was rather heavily dressed, more than normal —Eddie said something about her being lit up like a Christmas tree. Well, she must have misunderstood him and thought he had said she looked 'lit,' because she turned on him and said, 'Not at all. There are some things one would rather not hear.' And she tossed her head and stomped into the other room, and believe me it was a very frigid night for the rest of the evening.

She sang very badly, probably as badly as I've ever heard her sing. She was furious. And the only thing I can think of is that she was in such a rage because she *was* a little tight. Someone asked me later, 'What happened out there?' I told him I thought they thought she might have had a bit much to drink. He sort of giggled and said, 'Well, she is a bit later than she usually is, isn't she?' This was around midnight and she was supposed to have started around eleven. But that phrase—'There are some things one would rather not hear'—is one I've never forgotten, and it's become a catchword in my own household."

Once Mabel had settled in at the New Byline Room, which had been named the Mabel Mercer Room, the majority of her fans were happy to make the adjustment to new surroundings. By this time, her reputation as a singer's singer was thoroughly in place, and some of her listeners came not just to enjoy but also to learn. The pianist Van Cliburn was among them. Interviewed on television in Moscow after his victory in the Tchaikovsky Competition, he said that Mabel was one of the three greatest popular singers in America, along with Sinatra and Bobby Short.[19] But she was still largely unknown to the wider public, for she had recorded very little.

George Cory (who wrote "I Left My Heart in San Francisco") was pianist in residence at the New Byline Room, and he and his partner, arranger Douglass Cross, became good friends with Mabel. Cross, who worked at radio station WNYC, believed that Mabel needed some kind of management, which she did not have because she was averse to such businesslike things. He persuaded her to allow him to act in that capacity.

"Mabel is the only one Doug ever managed," says Bob Adams, who was then an announcer at WNYC. "He and George were very close to Billie Holiday, but they were not involved in her management. For Doug, it was a labor of love. He just wanted an association with her and he felt that he could do something for her. Perhaps he felt that not enough was being done, that she was such a well-kept secret among a small group of people in Manhattan."

Mabel was very fond of Cory and Cross—Bob Adams

remembers seeing her often at their apartment in Brooklyn Heights—and she was delighted that Cross wanted to help her. Once she had accepted his offer, he proceeded to negotiate on her behalf her first major recording contract with Atlantic Records. Bob Adams recalls that the terms of the contract were some kind of record in themselves. "I don't know the sums involved, but he negotiated with Neshuhi Ertegun, who with his brother Ahmet had founded the company, for a contract that was precedent-setting. Doug was very proud of having done that, and of course Mabel entirely deserved it, although that doesn't mean you always get it. Douglass was quite close to Neshuhi, and I am sure that helped."

This led to the release of *Mabel Mercer Sings Cole Porter*, on which she was accompanied by the dual pianos of Stan Freeman and her old friend Cy Walter. It contained "Experiment," "Looking at You," "After You," "I'm Ashamed That Women Are So Simple," and "It's Delovely," among other Porter songs. Although it is considered the best album Mabel ever recorded, it did not make the Hit Parade, but Neshuhi and Ahmet Ertegun were willing to continue the company's new relationship with Mabel.

Mabel renewed her relationship with her former accompanist Sam Hamilton around that time. In Peter Conway's recollection, it was Mabel who made the first move, although Hamilton was in a mood to take her up on it. "After about a year, year-and-a-half, Sam decided that the sporting goods business took more work and a lot greater investment than he thought it would, and he kind of got disillusioned with it. And at about that time Mabel, I guess, had decided she needed him more than she thought she did, so she wrote him and begged him to come back. And he did." Sam Hamilton remained with Mabel until he became gravely ill in the early 1960s.

In late 1957, Atlantic issued *The Art of Mabel Mercer*, a double album consisting primarily of previously recorded songs—Alec Wilder's "While We're Young" and "Goodbye John" (from a musical that had folded out of town), Bart Howard's "The First Warm Day in May" and "Let Me Love You" (also from a musical that had folded out of town), and Cy Walter's "Some Fine Day" and "The End of a Love Affair." "The photo on the jacket was taken in the New Byline Room," says Peter Conway. "Mabel is in a red dress and Sam is playing, and George Cory and Doug Cross are sitting in the audience."

The album did not sell well. Without being able to see Mabel—the wink of the eye, the slight raising of the eyebrow, the expressiveness of the hands—the listener could not appreciate it. "I don't think Mabel was a recording artist," says Julius Monk. "I don't think Bobby Short is, nor Hugh Shannon was, nor a great number of people who are charismatic in person. They have a great empathy for their audiences—and Mabel especially, sitting eyeball to eyeball, or glottis to glottis, if you'd like." Entertainer Ronny Whyte first saw her in person at the Byline Room. "I was in the Air Force, then, stationed in New England, and someone suggested that we go to see her. I'd heard a couple of her records and had thought, 'I don't know what that is,' but this person insisted I go and so I went and I was just devastated. She just wasted me. But I had to see her before I understood what she had."

Unfortunately, the New Byline Room did not stay open long—anyone who knows the nightclub business also knows that there is little rhyme or reason to why a place does well or does poorly, or why a successful club in one spot cannot seem to move that success with it to another location. Mabel's letter to Bricktop of May 16, 1958, refers to her staying at the club only into the summer of that year.

Mabel went almost immediately into the RSVP Room, though she made arrangements on Monday nights in October to do something different. This included a series of concerts at the Cherry Lane Theatre in Greenwich Village. *Monday Nights at Nine* was the brainchild of Gus Schirmer, Jr., of the music publishing family, who ordinarily presented *The Boy Friend* at the theater. Billed as "a series of theatrical diversions," the experimental program was inaugurated by Mabel, who agreed to two consecutive Monday night performances. Wrote the reviewer for *Variety* after the first: "It's a tough assignment to hold down a stage for more than two hours with nothing more than a songbag, a staircase, a red velvet chair and a lectern for props and a piano and bass assist in the pit but Miss Mercer does it with ease. . . . And at a flat $4.60 admission, sans booze, it's a neat trick in any promoter's book."[20]

While the Cherry Lane Theatre was a departure from the intimate boîtes in which she was accustomed to performing, Mabel somehow managed to make the place seem small and intimate. Beata Gray remembers that Mabel came across beautifully: "It was a late-night concert, and I took a friend from out of town. I had taken this friend to hear Mabel at Tony's once, and Mabel hadn't been singing very well that night and this friend of mine was *not* enchanted. But then I took her to this concert, and afterward she said, 'Now, I hear it. I see it. I hear it.' "

But the place for Mabel was a small club, and the RSVP Room became her new "home." She stayed there for two years.

She took the club's name seriously, and graciously responded to every request from a patron, as had been her habit always. Respect for her audience was a hallmark with Mabel. One time at the RSVP Room, she asked a woman in the audience what she wanted her to sing, and the woman asked for "Melancholy Baby." This song is the subject of an old show-business joke: an entertainer can spend hundreds of dollars to buy new material but someone will always ask for "Melancholy Baby." That night at the RSVP Room, according to Mabel, "The orchestra nearly died. Sing 'Melancholy Baby'? They were derisive, thought it was a joke. But this song meant a lot to this lady, so I sat at her table and sang 'Melancholy Baby' just as a song, which it is, and not a joke."[21]

On another occasion, a young man who was a regular customer arrived with a friend who kept interrupting her with, "Sing an Irish song! Sing an Irish song!" Mabel later recalled, "I said, 'Let me finish this one I'm doing.' When I finished, he insisted on singing 'When Irish Eyes Are Smiling,' or something. I've forgotten. He was having a good time. I didn't mind. The next night the young man came back and apologized for his friend. 'It's all right,' I told him. 'The man was feeling good and just wanted to hear some of his own Irish music.' The young man answered, 'But he's not even Irish! He's a Dane!' "[22]

Bart Howard was especially pleased that Mabel was at the RSVP Room. He'd been working at the Blue Angel across the street since 1952, and hadn't minded traveling to see her two or three times a week after his work was done at two or two-thirty A.M., whether it be at the old Byline Room on East 52nd Street or the New Byline Room on West 56th. But now he simply had to go across the street. "I went every night, of course. And Mabel would come to dinner, because I lived right next door to the Blue Angel. I was still taking songs to her, but by that time other people were singing my songs.

"When Mabel died, the news releases said that I had written 'Fly Me to the Moon' for Mabel and that Mabel was the first person to sing it and that she had made a big success of it. Now, I had never told anybody who sang it first because at the time I wrote that Mabel had an accompanist, Sam Hamilton, who was never getting around to learning the songs and it wasn't such a special song that Mabel would learn it at that time. Anyway, when I saw the news releases, I called up Mabel's publicist and told him he shouldn't have done that. It was unfair to all the other singers; and anyway, some singers won't sing a song if they think someone else has already sung it. Actually, the first person who ever sang it was Felicia Sanders, who was at the Blue Angel when I wrote it. It was just by accident— she was crazy about it when she first saw it. In the meantime, I had become friends with Johnny Mathis. We went together a lot to see Mabel, and I was feeding him because in those days he didn't have a lot of money, and he recorded songs, and some of them were mine, and that's what got me out of the Blue Angel because I finally made some money."

During her first few months at the RSVP Room, Mabel

began work on a new album for Atlantic, called *Once in a Blue Moon*. (*Midnight at Mabel Mercer's*, the second album under the new contract, had been released earlier.) George Cory, composer and pianist who had shared piano accompaniment duties with Sam Hamilton as well as doing the arranging on the *Midnight* album, left the piano playing to Sam Hamilton on this one, while he did the arrangements and also conducted the orchestra. It was the first time that Mabel had been backed by strings on an album. Shirley Fleming, who attended one of the three recording sessions for an article on Mabel for *Hi-Fi Music at Home* magazine, described the session:

"It was an evening date, partly because that was the only time many of the musicians were available, and partly because of the peculiar but understandable affinity which entertainers have for the hours after nightfall. Miss Mercer arrived dressed for the club, which she would go on to after perhaps four hours of concentrated singing into Atlantic's mike. The musicians appeared in less formal garb, took off their coats . . . and settled down to work. . . . Most of the players were from among the finest of New York's classical artists—members of the Symphony of the Air, the New York Woodwind Quintet, and other such organizations—men rarely involved in producing pop records, but attracted to the idea on Miss Mercer's account.

"George Cory, one of the country's most talented young composers and pianists, arranged and conducted the songs to be recorded (he and Mabel have worked together for years and she sings many of his songs). He had scored with a care for instrumentation which gave the accompaniments an almost chamber-music-like quality. . . . But instrumentation, in such an undertaking as this, was only half the battle, for accompanying so individual a singer as Mabel Mercer with so large a group of players raised problems of its own. The accompanists must follow the singer in tempo and phrasing—a relatively clear task for a solitary piano but a sizable hurdle for an orchestra. Pianist Sam Hamilton, who accompanies Mabel in her nightly appearances and has done so for nearly ten years, glides easily into successive songs at a nod from the singer, and seems to know as well as she does just where she will hold back on a note or speed up a phrase. Mr. Cory's assembled players had to learn to forget the precise time-values of the notes before them, and rely almost entirely on the conductor's signals—and he, in turn, had to take his cue from the soloist. Not a simple business, to be sure, but eventually accomplished after a number of dry runs, followed by a number of takes, followed by play-backs and more takes. And at various points during these procedures an old tradition was observed which is part of every Mercer recording session: the serving of champagne.

"The success of the session, at which the instrumentalists saw their music for the first time, depended in part on how many difficulties Mr. Cory and Miss Mercer were able to anticipate and iron out ahead of time. They had worked together closely during the preceding weeks, Mr. Cory playing his arrangements at the piano and describing the instrumentation, so that the first performance with the orchestra would not be disconcertingly novel to the soloist. Mabel, on her part, indicated tempo preferences and occasionally suggested changes in the accompaniment, preceded gently by, 'That's lovely, dear, but . . .' After years of collaboration, they understood each other well, and George Cory's arrangements are tailor-made for her, with considerable musical activity and color in the accompaniments which, however, never cover up the voice or detract from it.

"After such groundwork, the evening date was almost guaranteed to be a success, and such it was. Shortly after 10 o'clock, Atlantic's president Neshuhi Ertegun walked out of the control room to say, 'Very nice, Mabel, very nice indeed,' the musicians began to pack up their instruments, and Mabel left for the club where the night's work awaited her."[23]

It was at the RSVP Room that Will Craik finally got to know Mabel, although he had been a fan for years. "I was born and brought up in Boston," says Craik. "A friend of mine there had some of Mabel's records, and I loved her voice. This friend

121

said she often played clubs in New York, and I always made up my mind that if I ever got to New York and she was playing anywhere, I was going to go and see her. Later on, I did move to New York, worked on Wall Street as an administrator handling back office, clerical help, and one day I just happened to see in the paper that she was playing. The first time I saw her she was at Tony's. I just went and heard her, I didn't meet her then. I went to a couple of other places she played—the Byline Room, the New Byline Room. But then she got to the RSVP and that was quite near where I lived, and I stopped by many times. I used to work late in the office and on the way home I'd stop in there and get a bite to eat and a couple of drinks, and I'd sit and listen to her. And I guess she noticed me, coming so often, because I turned around one time from the bar and there she was, sitting at my right hand. We got talking and she said she'd noticed me coming in very often and she was happy I liked her music. We got to be great friends. So I used to tell people she picked me up in a bar."

Craik in fact became one of Mabel's frequent escorts to dinner and shows. "She liked Goldie's on Lexington Avenue. It was owned by Goldie Hawkins, a pianist from Louisiana. A lot of the show business people hung out there, and she liked it because when they went there they were on. Art Carney would think nothing of getting up and going over to the piano and playing, and people would gather round and sing. You could see Ethel Merman at the bar, if you wanted to see Ethel Merman. Ed McMahon used to come in. It was just a hangout, and Goldie knew everybody in the business. Dorothy Kilgallen used to come in there. She was no big favorite of ours. She didn't write mean things about Mabel, but she did about some of Mabel's friends, and they would get very annoyed about that. She also liked Michael's Pub—we'd go to dinner there— both locations. Once in a while somebody would call and say, 'Would you like to come to dinner here or there?' and we would go. But she was not adventurous. She liked to go where she knew she would get certain things, and she liked the old familiar places.

"The biggest compliment she ever paid me, though we never discussed it, was the time she called me up, it was a Sunday, and I said, 'What do you want to do, go to the chinks and the flicks [a Chinese restaurant and a movie]?' And she said, 'No, I want to go to a cocktail party. Will you take me?' I said, 'Well, sure, I'm not doing anything.' It seems a gentleman from Atlanta or Washington, D.C., or somewhere was giving a cocktail party at the St. Regis, in one of the suites, and we went, and I was the only white in the place. It never dawned on me until somebody pointed it out to me. And it never entered Mabel's mind that I might be bothered by this, because I wasn't, not at all."

Naturally, Mabel told Craik all about Blakely, her upstate home, and Craik, who enjoyed the country, listened with great interest. "And she just suggested that she could use a hired hand at her country house, and we just always seemed to be on the same wavelength, so I started coming up on weekends—came up about *every* weekend—and on vacations and days off. Sometimes she wouldn't come up with me, because she would be playing somewhere and she'd have to come up a day later or something. Harry and I would come up, and she'd come a day later, and we'd meet the train, Harry and I. Sometimes Harry would drive us up, and we'd all come together. I used to take vacations a day at a time."

It was a rare weekend when they were at the farm in Red Rock alone, for Mabel invited everyone she knew to spend weekends there. "She kind of scheduled people," says Will Craik, "all kinds of people. And Harry would have conniption fits. The place wasn't the sort of place you'd associate with Mabel Mercer on the stage—we called it 'Ramshackle Manor'—and Harry thought this was ruining her image. She couldn't care less. He used to say, 'I'm embarrassed for her.' But she'd say, 'They take me as I am,' and they always did."

For a saver like Mabel, it didn't take long for the house with its warren of little rooms to become cluttered. For instance, remembers Craik, "She would hoard things like little transparent slivers of soap; she would crush them into a ball and

123

save them. I would say, 'You don't have to do that; the stores are full of soap.' And she'd say, 'Oh, you Americans are so wasteful.'

"And then I'd be cooking something and I'd go to the spice rack. She had a metal cabinet with three or four shelves in there with nothing in it but cans of spices, but you couldn't find anything—they were just thrown in there. I would say, 'I'm looking for cinnamon, or nutmeg.' She'd say, 'Oh, it's in there, dear.' I'd spend half an hour looking for it, and she'd say, 'Oh, no matter, dear, we'll get some tomorrow.' Then finally one day I was up here and she was not, and I said for once I'm going to organize that thing alphabetically and find out what we've got in there, and there must have been six tins of everything. And I remember telling her, 'We are so wasteful!'

"She could not throw anything out. Leftovers from dinner or something, a little dab, and she'd put it in a dish and put it in the refrigerator and then forget it was in there. I'd tell her, 'I want to clean that up,' and she'd say, 'Oh, isn't that a lovely color blue, in that bowl.' She used to drive Harry crazy, because rather than just throw it in the garbage she would throw it on the ground. This was compost. And then she used to wonder why there were so many mosquitoes and flies and things around. She would take tea grounds, tea leaves, and they always went out onto the ground, and Harry used to go *crazy* because he used to like to sun himself out on the back terrace, and the flies would buzz around his head. But she'd say, 'This belongs to the earth, it's good for the earth, good for the earth.' "

CHAPTER

VI

MABEL OUT
OF
FASHION

THE YEAR MABEL MERCER turned sixty, a few students from the black North Carolina Agricultural & Technical College decided to sit in at a local Woolworth's. Within a few months, the sit-in movement had spread like wildfire across the South. Building on the momentum of the Montgomery bus boycott of two years earlier, the student sit-in movement led to the founding of the Student Nonviolent Coordinating Committee (SNCC), which individually and in concert with the Southern Christian Leadership Conference, led by the Reverend Martin Luther King, Jr., and the older Congress of Racial Equality (CORE), launched a full-blown civil rights movement in the United States. As a woman who was half black and who had suffered her share of discrimination in her adopted country, Mabel Mercer might have been expected to join in. But she did not. She was not political, although she followed current events

125

closely. In fact, Mabel Mercer, U.S. citizen, never even exercised her right to vote.

One suspects that her one and only attempt to register turned her off the whole affair. Recalls Will Craik, "One time we said, 'Would you like us to take you down to register to vote?' She said, 'No, thank you. I've had experience with your voter registration.' She explained to me that one time when she was in Florida, visiting Kelsey Pharr's people—it may have been for his funeral [Pharr died in 1964]—somebody asked her to register. So, she went to register, and they gave her a very hard time—'Gal, can you read? Gal, can you write?' Well, that was enough for Mabel. She told me, 'So, I have never bothered. I could read and write better than the fellow who was asking me the questions.' She walked out.

"She wasn't at all interested in the civil rights movement per se, the militant type," says Will Craik. "She liked Dr. King and was very much in favor of equal rights—she wasn't the Uncle Tom type. She just wasn't militant about it. Once or twice they asked her to join a program—I can't remember the circumstances. There were some people like Langston Hughes, I remember, and some very active, vigorous people, who wanted her to get involved, but she just didn't want to. I think she considered it an American problem—she still considered herself very British, and the problem didn't exist over there.

"She had her own ideas about race, and sometimes they didn't make much sense. She wouldn't like it when anyone pointed out racial differences, and as a rule such differences didn't even enter her mind. But sometimes she would point them out herself. She knew this singer named Elisabeth Welch [who introduced "Charleston" in the 1923 musical Runnin' Wild] over in London, and when she heard that people were going over to England she would ask if they would drop in and see Elisabeth and say hello for her. And Mabel would always add, 'But she's colored, you know.' And I'd always say, 'Now, who's the racist?' And she would look at me as if she didn't know what I was talking about."

For Mabel, the Sixties was not the time of the civil rights struggle but of her own struggle to survive. After two years at the RSVP Room on the East Side, she again faced a time when she had no permanent place to perform. In January 1960 she began an eight-week stint at the King Arthur Room, which was part of a jazz club on Broadway called the Roundtable, but this was not her idea of performing. The thousand dollars a week salary notwithstanding, there wasn't enough time to develop a loyal following in the place.

Even Mabel could see that the nightclub era was waning, and in the late winter-early spring of 1960, sixty-year-old Mabel realized that she would have to make some effort to attract a wider audience. Until this time, she had rarely ventured out of New York City. Her 1954 appearance in Chicago's Blue Angel had been the one, unusual exception. Douglass Cross had urged her to perform outside New York, and in April 1958 she had flown to Atlanta for two invitation-only concerts at El Morocco on Peachtree Street. The performances were sold out. Bob Adams recalls, "It was a great success; affluent people there kind of took her up. She had marvelous publicity, and they adored her." But she had turned down numerous offers to go back.

Two years later, Cross approached Mabel with the idea of an extended trip that would include engagements in both Chicago and San Francisco. Bob Adams remembers that Mabel was reluctant to go. "In the beginning, she didn't want to go, and Doug said, 'Oh, Mabel, you've *got* to go. Come on, you've *got* to go!' " Eventually she gave in, and when her engagement at the King Arthur Room ended, Mabel took off for points West.

Actually, Mabel had dreamed for years of one day traveling across the United States, and had often talked about it after she had got her first car. Harry accompanied her, and they drove back from San Francisco.

Mabel's comparatively extended trip included a month-long engagement at the Chicago Playboy Club's Library, where she inaugurated its intimate, fifty-seat After Hours Shows, as well as a stint at the hungry I in San Francisco where, after Mabel's opening seven days, the management built a small, carpeted show room for her, obviously constructed to her specifications. She performed there until September 15.

On the way back east from San Francisco, she and Harry stopped off at a number of places and made many new friends, all of whom were invited to Red Rock if they ever passed that way.

As it happened, one couple took her up on the invitation, which occasioned one of the few times that Will Craik ever saw Mabel angry. "They were a young couple," says Craik. "They had treated Mabel and Harry to dinner out there. The wife was from the Hamilton Beach appliance family, and this was her second husband. She was a very attractive redhead, and that was a danger signal right there, because Harry liked redheads. Well, they came up, and Mabel decided she would make some Welsh cakes. These were a famous treat she made—like scones. She made them on top of the stove, on a griddle, and she ran out of something—butter or something. And Harry said he would go into town and get her some butter, and the woman thought she'd go with him. And Mabel sort of looked, but said nothing. And they went, and they were gone for four hours! Mabel was fooling with the dough and saying, 'What are they doing? *Churning* that butter?' When they came back in, she blew up. She just told the woman, 'Please go pack your bags and leave.' Harry just took off and went to his room. Mabel somehow seemed to think that this was not really Harry's fault. She found him so irresistible, so everybody else must, too."

This was not the only instance of Harry's eye wandering. According to Will Craik, he had a long-term relationship with a woman in Rochester, New York, whom he visited on occasion. "Mabel called Rochester 'Captain's Paradise.' Remember the old Alec Guiness movie? I'd come up and say, 'Where is Harry?' and she'd say, 'Oh, he's up in Captain's Paradise.' She didn't let it bother her.

"He always told us he had a doctor up there, a 'specialist.'

But as Mabel said, 'He never said a specialist in *what*, dear.' He always drove up, but one time Mabel got very sick, and Harry had the car, and that's the last time Harry took the car up to Captain's Paradise. From then on, we'd take him to the station, and he'd spend eight hours on the train going up there."

After her "coast-to-coast" tour, Mabel Mercer returned to find that there was very little work for nightclub singers. In fact, nightclubs just about died during the 1960s, felled by a combination of factors, not the least of which was television. People preferred to stay home at night and because of this a lot of clubs folded. When they did venture out, rock 'n' roll concerts were the most popular form of live entertainment. It was the era of the Beatles and the Rolling Stones. The stars who wanted to see and be seen went to the Peppermint Lounge, not the Byline Room. It was a time when youth was celebrated, and when nearly everyone, of whatever age, wanted to seem young and "with it." That meant not going to some tiny boîte where a sixty-year-old singer sang ironic tunes without blare or pizzazz. Says Julius Monk, "We don't have a tradition of diseuses here, as they do in Paris, and we don't have the loyalty that the English have to elderly citizens, which Mabel had become. As a consequence, she was really quite rare, the first of her breed." And not doing too well at it.

About this period, which lasted around three years, Mabel said, "They were making too much noise to listen to me sing; they wanted to dance."[1] But her dismissal aside, it was quite a painful time for her. "You know," says Rosetta LeNoire, "she didn't realize that she was very fortunate to work as much as she did in those days. None of us worked like that, but she didn't realize that. Coming from Europe [where black performers rarely had trouble getting work], she didn't really know what it was like for black performers in the States. That [not being able to find work] was way beneath her, whereas the rest of us had already been conditioned to it—we hated it, but what could we do? We were in America and this was it for us."

129

Had Mabel been making big money in earlier years, she might have welcomed the work hiatus; but Mabel did not have substantial savings on which to fall back. The reported thousand dollars a week she made at the King Arthur Room of the Roundtable for eight weeks led some people to believe erroneously that she could afford not to work for a few years. "She was basically a very poor woman," says Peter Conway. "I never believed it at first, but Sam [Hamilton, Mabel's pianist], finally convinced me. He said, 'Everything she has in the world is in that farm and in the clothes on her back and in her car.' I guess she was working for very little money all those years and never managed to save anything at all."

Friends helped her. Alec Wilder, who wrote the music for the short film *The Sand Castle*, was no doubt responsible for Mabel's being cast as the Voice of the Shell, which earned her a bit of money. (The film, written, produced, and directed by Jerome Hill, contained eighteen songs by Wilder and also featured Wilder as The Fisherman.) People who wish not to be mentioned here gave her money; some of them, not wanting to hurt her feelings, waited until Christmas or her birthday to do so. On such occasions, they felt they could give her fairly substantial cash gifts. Says Will Craik, "Joe Carstairs helped her sometimes, but I don't know if it was annually or not. Mabel didn't discuss finance." On occasion a well-meaning acquaintance was too obvious about wanting to help her financially, and Mabel was offended.

Conway recalls that an East Side friend of Mabel's was going to give her a kind of benefit. "I remember I received this very formal invitation in the mail: Mabel was going to sing again at a very private garden party. It would cost me twenty-five dollars to go 'for the benefit of Mabel.' About two or three weeks later I got a phone call that the thing was canceled completely. I called Sam, and he said she'd heard that the guy was doing this and planning to give her the money, and she was furious that invitations had gone out saying 'for the benefit of Mabel.' She did not want anybody to know, or even to think, that she was in any way needy or not sitting on top of the world."

Will Craik knew better, of course. "There was no place for her to play, and so she came up here—she had the house and she stayed here and she was very happy. Her favorite pastime, and I can see her now, was sitting in her kitchen at the foot of the stairs in front of the stove. It was an old, cast-iron, wood-burning stove, pot-bellied. We had found it in the barn —Adde's son, Peter (son of Mabel's neighbor Adelaide Wallin-Beach), and I—and we'd cleaned it up and brought it in. She liked nothing better than to stare into the fire. She could do it for hours on end. She would build a fire in that pot-bellied stove, and she had a chair near there, and she'd pull it up and sit in it. I would come downstairs in the morning, and she would have been up ahead of me and built a fire, and she would just stare into it. She also loved the fireplace in the living room. On a hot August day she'd have logs in the fireplace, blazing away. I used to ask her, 'What do you see in there?' She'd say, 'Things you'd never dream of, lad.'"

She gardened, she fed the birds. Says Father Lee Smith, who met Mabel through Will Craik and who also became a good friend, "When you went up to Mabel's in winter, you never had to worry about sliding on the ice because it was impregnated with birdseed. The birds were not afraid—they knew they were okay at Mabel's, even with the cats. She loved her cats, but they'd better keep away from the birds." She cared for her animals. She read. "She was very interested in space exploration," recalls Craik. "She'd say, 'The only thing I don't understand, dear, is why are we up there trying to discover new worlds when we can't get along with each other in this one?' She loved reading about the astronauts. She had a lot of science fiction in the house, and she loved science fiction movies. She loved Edgar Cayce—everything he wrote was written in stone—'It's going to come true, dear, it's going to come true.' There was an earthquake once, and I remember her saying, 'Edgar Cayce predicted it.' I know from other people that once

131

or twice she sneaked off to séances in the city. She had the normal superstitions that entertainers have, but she didn't make a big deal about superstitions."

She did very little housekeeping, probably because the idea of even trying to clean through that cluttered little warren of rooms was defeating. "She had a collection of owls," says Craik. "She thought owls were good luck, and of course this solved everyone's problem—you want to give Mabel something, you give her an owl. She had them on the mantel above the fireplace, and they sat there year after year and just collected layer upon layer of dust. Maybe once a year I would get to the point where I couldn't stand it any longer and I'd take them down and dust them off. She'd say, 'I would have done that had you given me time.' I'd say, 'You only had ten years. How much time do you want?' "

Mabel's housekeeping was a subject on which Harry Beard constantly carped, to little avail. "Mabel hardly cared about housekeeping. The bare minimum, she could get by with," says Craik. "She'd rather be out doing things. Harry was fastidious, but of course he would never lift a finger. I remember one time Mabel and I had gone into Chatham, and when we came back Harry was waiting at the back door for us. Mabel was hurrying. She thought there might be a phone call or something. And Harry said, 'I've been waiting for you to get back. I've got to get into the refrigerator.' Mabel said, 'Well, go ahead.' 'I can't. One of your dogs has thrown up right in front of it.'

"Up here in the country you have little tiny mice; they get into everything. Harry couldn't stand them—they'd drive him up a wall. He'd hear one in the cupboard or something and go crazy. I don't know how many hundreds of mousetraps he bought—he had them in all the cupboards and all over the place—and Mabel was scared to death one of the animals would catch a paw in one of them. As fast as he'd put them in there, she'd go around throwing them out.

"It got very boring, his constant complaining. If it wasn't the mice, it was the cats. 'These damn cats, this damn cat hair,

these cats have got to go.' Mabel wouldn't say much until he
threatened the animals. Then she'd just look at him and say,
'You'll go first.' And the minute she threatened anything like
that, he backed off. He had a good thing going, and he knew
it.

"Mabel once told me that they used to hold hands so they
wouldn't swing at each other. She didn't mean that literally,
though. There were times when they would get along very well
until Harry would start in on her about the housekeeping. Over
the years, she had come to depend on him very heavily and she
always felt a sense of obligation because of the messy separation
from his wife. Mabel once said, 'He went through an awful lot
for me.' "

In the early 1960s, when Mabel wasn't working, Harry
took over from Douglass Cross the duties of being her manager.
He served in that capacity for some years, although her friends
could not see what managing he did for her and wondered who
else or what else he'd ever managed. They had heard that at
one point he had managed a restaurant in Philadelphia. If nothing else, he attended to things like balancing checkbooks and
signing contracts and sundry other business matters, all of which
Mabel thoroughly detested and for which she was grateful to
Harry. Another advantage was that finally Harry had a title,
which made it easier for both of them to explain who he was.

By this time, Mabel was free to marry him, had he wished
to. Kelsey Pharr was dead. Recalls Will Craik, "She went down
to the funeral when Kelsey died—I understand he died quite
young. She used to say, 'I saw him when we got married and
I went to his funeral, but that's it.' We used to tease her, call
her the Widow Pharr." But after all their time together, there
didn't seem to be much sense in getting married then. "Anyway," remembers Craik, "Harry had an eye for the ladies and
was not the marrying kind. I think his was a case of once burnt,
twice shy. I think Mabel would at least have liked the opportunity to marry him, but as she once put it to me, 'He never
did me the honor of asking for my hand.' " Mabel and Harry

went on as they had for years, going their separate ways together. While Mabel stayed up in Red Rock, Harry remained in the apartment in New York, visiting the farm mostly on weekends.

During her time of enforced retirement, Mabel had no choice but to collect unemployment insurance, which she regarded as being on the dole. Craik recalls, "It embarrassed her, and she felt as if she was taking welfare or something. I had to convince her—you paid for this, every time you got a paycheck you were paying; this is insurance, not welfare. She finally agreed to go into Hudson so she could register and collect it. It was very little—I don't know why the sum of seventy-five dollars comes to mind, I don't think it was that much. And it took everything I could come up with to convince her that she had a right to collect it. I think what did the trick was when I told her I'd heard stories on the news about Groucho Marx driving up to the unemployment office in Hollywood in his Rolls-Royce. When I told her that, she said, 'Well, if he can do it, I can do it.' But I had a tough time."

Even with the small unemployment checks she collected, Mabel continued to have a difficult time making ends meet. She kept the apartment on 110th Street in Manhattan—friends suggest that she did so primarily because she couldn't face cleaning it out. Of course, that would have included cleaning out Harry, who was living there, although according to Will Craik he didn't want anyone to know it. There were the taxes to pay on the Chatham property, and then there was the matter of food. Says Craik, "She got depressed about not having any money to do anything with. Not for money itself, but because there were things she wanted to do and she couldn't do them. There was the house, which she was always adding on to, and the animals, and the neighborhood children. Food was the last thing on her list, but it was a necessity. I remember one time I came up and I'd just got out of the car when she said, 'Oh, we gotta go shopping.' She had a box of cornflakes in her house, period—she was down to that.

"That happened over and over again. I'd drive up, get out of the car, and she'd say, 'Oh, thank God you're here. We must go shopping,' and we'd go to the supermarket and she would get a cart and make a beeline for the pet-food counter. And she would load that cart up with cat food and dog food, and then we had to go find the frozen horsemeat. She had four dogs plus any that dropped in from the neighborhood. There were two of her own and the neighbor's two dogs, Brownie and Nellie —they just kept coming up, and she kept feeding them. Finally, Mr. Macready [Don Macready, the dogs' owner] said, 'You know, they spend more time at your house than they do at mine, you might just as well have them.' So she took them. And she didn't believe anybody could take proper care of a cat except Mabel. I've only known one other person like this, but with her, the animals came first. You took care of them before you fed the humans. They were like her children. Anyway, not until she had the shopping cart brimful with that stuff did she think about us. She'd say, 'Now, do you mind, dear, if I put some things in there for us to eat?' "

Fortunately for Mabel, her period of unemployment lasted for only about three years. By April 1963 she was ensconced at Downstairs at the Upstairs, where her old friend from Paris, Julius Monk, was the artistic director, and in January 1964 she began celebrating her golden anniversary in show business in the club's appropriately Edwardian decor that invoked images of Wallis and the Duke and of a gentler time. Thanks to some savvy publicity releases from the club, she received her first national media coverage in several years when *Newsweek* devoted a small piece to her.

Mabel aficionados, of course, did not need to read *Newsweek* to find out where she was appearing. Phyllis King Day, a publicist, knew where Mabel lived and had written to Mabel asking when and where she was next appearing. She learned that Mabel was at Downstairs at the Upstairs, and arranged to take friends there for dinner and to hear Mabel sing on January 29, 1964. "I had the opportunity to introduce myself, as I had

135

written to ask where she was next opening," says Day. "When asked was I there for something special besides hearing her, I said yes, I was celebrating my upcoming birthday. Asked if it was that night, I said it was the next Monday. She replied, 'Why, that's February 3—*my* birthday,' so we were off to a good start. And I still have the telegram she sent me that day, wishing me a happy one!! In years we were only two apart."[2]

Allen Carter, who had been in California for several years and had not seen Mabel during that time, returned to New York in 1964. "I was in Sardi's one night for dinner, and I asked Vincent Sardi where Mabel was singing and he told me. We had theater tickets for that night, and I suggested that we go to see Mabel after the theater. As we walked into Downstairs at the Upstairs, I asked the maître d', 'Is Miss Mercer singing?' He said, 'No, she's sitting right over there.' Well, I went over. I tapped her on the shoulder and said, 'Excuse me, Miss Mercer, may I have your autograph?' And she turned around and smiled and then she got up and threw her arms around me and kissed me all over. And when the time came to sing, she got up and did all the old songs from Tony's in the Forties. She stumbled a little bit over the words, but it had been a long time.

"By that time I had stopped acting and was doing some writing, and Mabel said, 'Look, if you're going to write you've got to get out and meet people. Come with me here, come with me there. So and so is going to be here, so and so is going to be there. I will introduce you. You have got to know these people.' We went all over, and she introduced me to people wherever we went. Once in a great while I could return the favor and introduce her to someone from the Coast that she didn't know. I took her to see *The Subject Was Roses* with Jack Albertson, and we went backstage and I introduced her. Of course everybody knew who Mabel was. We'd walk down the street and people would say, 'Oh, there goes Mabel Mercer.'

"And then I took her once to see *Oh What a Lovely War*. It was a male show brought over from England and Victor Spinelli had the male lead and I knew Victor. Afterward we went to Sardi's and who should come in but Victor Spinelli. He came over and met Mabel, and then I had the whole cast, or at least the principals, over to the Downstairs at the Upstairs, so they could hear Mabel.

"I ran into Hermione Gingold after I came back from California, and I said, 'What are you doing for dinner? We'll drop over and see Mabel.' And her eyes lit up, and she said, 'You know, I will go out to dinner with you *only* because you're going to take me to see Mabel afterwards.' This was normal for Mabel's friends."

Recalls the artist Beata Gray, "When she was singing at Downstairs at the Upstairs, I used to go there alone—walk in there at midnight or something. She would always seat me with someone else, so I wouldn't be sitting alone. I painted a portrait of her—I don't know where it is—it hung in a couple of the clubs she sang in. I've got a small black-and-white photo of the painting; it was of Mabel singing at Downstairs at the Upstairs."

While at Downstairs at the Upstairs Mabel recorded another album, with a new record company. Atlantic had not issued an album of hers since 1959, but in 1964 Decca was willing to do so. *The Magic of Mabel Mercer*, released in the early fall of 1964, was arranged by Ralph Burns and included Bart Howard's "Year After Year," Bob Merrill's "Mira," Cy Coleman's and Carolyn Leigh's "I've Got Your Number," Marvin Fisher's and Jack Segal's "Run to Love" and "Trouble Comes," Fran Landesmann's and Tommy Wolf's "Ballad of the Sad Young Men," and Gordon Jenkins's "This Is All I Ask." Reviewing the album in *Hi Fi/Stereo Review*, Gene Lees admitted that he had never seen Mabel in person—"an oversight I intend to correct as soon as possible"—but was less than hopeful about the potential sales of this latest album: "Bless her. May she long endure and continue to show us what it's all about. I hope this record sells, though I am somewhat doubtful. It seems we've never been able to give Miss Mercer anything approaching what she's given us."[3]

Mabel's complete "giving" to her audiences—to each individual listener—was so legendary that even one who had not seen her in person remarked on it. At no time was that generosity more evident, in the recollection of Lawrence Sharpe, than at Downstairs at the Upstairs on the night of October 15, 1964: "It was the evening of the day Cole Porter died. My date and I went to see her that evening, staying on after the first show. It was Miss Mercer's habit after a show to come and sit with different members of the audience, as if the entertainment was in her own living room. She came to our table and talked in generalities, and I asked her if she felt like singing a special song of Cole Porter's. She declined gracefully, saying that he was a very special friend of hers and she didn't think she would be able to sing one of his songs tonight. We, of course, understood.

"However, in the middle of the second set, after concluding a number, she turned to her accompanist and talked with him for a moment, and then turning back to the audience started in singing 'Ev'ry Time We Say Goodbye.' She made no announcement as to why she had chosen the song, no comment about Cole Porter, no comment about the request . . . but the poignancy of her choice and the manner in which she delivered it said it all."[4]

Mabel remained at Downstairs at the Upstairs for some two and a half years, with brief vacations in between. She spent some of the money she had earned there on the most extensive addition yet to the farm. It was two stories, with an office for Harry and a banistered deck with a glorious vista. Says Father Lee Smith, "It was a brand-new house, and I remember thinking, 'My God, she's not ready to give up yet! She's going on, she's going on for another sixty [years]!' " What Father Smith did not know at the time was that the lower story of the addition contained a bedroom and adjoining bath for Mabel so she would not have to go upstairs as often. By this time arthritis affected not only her hands but had also settled in her knees, making it difficult for her to climb stairs. Says Will Craik, "She had to literally crawl up the stairs." But she still had to "sing for her supper," as she put it, and so she returned to Downstairs at the Upstairs for the fall and then the spring, and another fall and another spring, the seasons at the club like the seasons of the trees on her farm in Red Rock. And this at a time when other people her age were thinking about retirement. Mabel Mercer seemed to be getting a second wind. Or perhaps it was simply that the national publicity long overdue her was finally coming her way.

In October 1965, *Life* magazine did a piece on her. It seemed a fitting historical moment, a time when common Americans were ready to appreciate her—they might not have heard her sing, but they liked her attitude. Commenting in the article about why people packed into Downstairs at the Upstairs three times a night to hear her, she said, "I guess I grow on 'em like a barnacle." In the wake of that article, suddenly there were people from outside the major metropolitan areas who not only had heard of her but wanted to hear her.

Recalls Rosetta LeNoire, "Even white people from the South who visited me, the moment I mentioned Mabel, said, 'Oh, please take me, I read about her in the magazine.' And I would take them and they felt—now get this, because it was amazing and it happened over and over and over again—when I would take a Southern white person down there to see her, they felt as if *they* had been given freedom. They were so excited and happy. I just couldn't get over it."

By 1966, however, the entertainment policy at Downstairs at the Upstairs changed, and although Mabel was invited for short engagements for several years afterward, she lost yet another "home" club. It is unlikely that Mabel's health had anything to do with the change, but Allen Carter remembers that she had put on considerable weight and, at least on one occasion, had to delay her set because of a stubborn nosebleed.

Her arthritis did not affect her singing, but the enlarged joints in her hands embarrassed her. Will Craik remembers that an artist did a portrait of her and she didn't like it because in it her hands looked large and gnarled. She preferred the work of

Lisa Rhana, whose pastel portrait of Mabel had been destroyed in the fire at the Byline Room. Rhana did two more studies of Mabel in 1964; neither included her hands. One, a red/brown Conte crayon drawing, was exhibited briefly, then inexplicably lost. Another, three faces of Mabel done in charcoal, survived.

After her long engagement at Downstairs at the Upstairs ended, Mabel made brief appearances at various clubs and remained based in the city. By this time the neighborhood on Central Park North was depressed. "She didn't like it," says Will Craik. "She'd say, 'Why don't [these people] go out and get a job? Anything is better than just sitting around.' The neighborhood really had gone downhill, and it was no place to be out on the street at three or four A.M. She always went back there after work in the morning. I usually drove her. We'd take a cab and I'd walk her to the door and to the elevator. Some nights I guess Harry took her. But she would always take a cab right to the door of her apartment, or somebody in the club would offer her a ride home."

For that matter, in Mabel's opinion, New York night life had also gone downhill. She wasn't the sort to bemoan such things often, but Will Craik remembers, "She used to talk about the good old days—'Oh, what ever happened to night life in this city?' She hated the business of being there a month or two, then coming back here to Red Rock for a while, and then going back down. She was always eager to work, and she worked pretty steadily. All of New York night life was that way— nobody stayed anyplace forever. There weren't that many supper clubs around anymore, or cabarets. And there were a lot of entertainers."

In addition to wishing to enjoy and benefit from what little there was left of New York night life, Mabel felt some responsibility to younger performers who had chosen the same road as she. Ronny Whyte, who had first heard Mabel in 1956 at the RSVP Room when he was in the Air Force, had arrived in New York in the early 1960s to seek his fortune as a club singer and pianist. "I think the first time she heard me was when

ris, 1932. Seated are
chael Farmer, Brick-
, Ramon Novarro,
abel, and Louis Cole.

Paris, early 1930s. Mabel
with Louis Cole, Brick-
top, and Alberta Hunter.

aris, late 1930s. Brick-
op is seated third from
eft.

Paris, 1938. Mabel and Jimmy Musso former headwaiter at Bricktop's and now owner of his own club, and Joh Hess.

Mabel, newly arrived in New York.

A 1941 portrait, inscribed to Bricktop.

At Hamilton College in upstate New York, late 1940s. Mabel, Bart Howard, and the student who arranged their visit to the campus.

...bel and Bart Howard with a scarf imprinted with one of his ...gs.

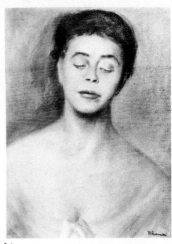

New York, 1946. The original of this Lisa Rhana portrait was destroyed by fire in the New Byline Room.

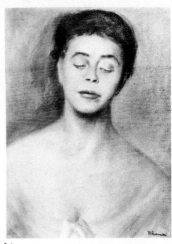

Nassau, Bahamas, late 1940s. With Joe Carstairs, Bart Howard, and friend.

Mabel, 1950s.

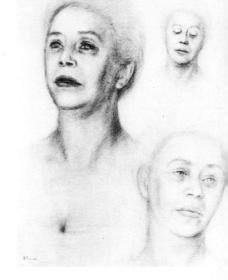

Lisa Rhana charcoal portrait, 1964.

Mabel with Harry Beard and Adelaide Wallin-Beach at Red Rock 1965.

Lisa Rhana pastel portrait, 1968.

Mabel and Bobby Short publicize their May, 1968 Town Hall concert.

South Carolina, 1972. Clockwise from bottom left are Buddy Barnes (Mabel's favorite accompanist), Bobby Short, jazz critic George Frazier, Alec Wilder, Bart Howard, singer Billie Mustin, and Billy Roy.

February 1975, Mabel's 75th birthday party. Entering the St. Regis Roof on the arm of Harry Beard.

Mabel receiving an honorary degree from Boston's Berklee College of Music, March 1975. With Alec Wilder (l) and Harry Beard, William Craik and Harry's sister, Pearl Lemert (r).

With Jimmy Lyon at the London Playboy Club, July 1977.

Mabel at Cafe Lefitte in Philadelphia.

Fall 1977. Mabel at Cleo, her last steady club engagement.

Mabel with her dogs and cats at her Red Rock farm.

Washington, D.C., February 23, 1983. Mabel receiving the Medal of Freedom from President Reagan.

Mabel, shortly before her death in 1984.

Bobby Short brought her to see me when I was working at this little place at Forty-fifth and Lexington called McEvoy's, and that was in 1964. I think Bart Howard worked there at one time. It was a funny little room but had a decent piano.

"In 1966 I opened at a place called Ramondo's and I was there for five years on and off. Somebody brought her in and she just loved the show and said she would recommend it to her friends. People would call her and ask where she was working, and she'd say, 'Well, I'm not working at the moment, but Ronny Whyte is at Ramondo's.' And so she would send people in, and she sort of became a regular there—she and Harry and Willie Craik and Muriel Finch used to all come in together. We'd see her almost once a week. And so we became very good friends. We went out to dinner a lot and I went up to her farm a couple of times.

"Although we were good friends, she was such a private person that I never pried, never asked her about Paris or her early life, although I would love to have heard about it. But one time we were driving up to her country place—a lady named Travis Hudson and I and a couple of other friends were driving up with her—and we were driving up the Taconic Parkway, and suddenly she started talking about it. We were just breathtaken, because we'd never heard her loosen up about it before. She was always so modest, felt that people really didn't care; and when she found out that we did, that we were just spellbound, she started weaving stories about Paris and Bricktop's, and we couldn't get enough of it.

"But that was a rare occasion. She didn't believe in talking about herself. She didn't believe in putting herself into her songs. One night Harry and Willie Craik and I were at the old Michael's Pub when it used to be just off Madison Avenue. We were having dinner before going to work, and Mabel was talking about how all the songs at the time were songs like 'I Did It My Way' and 'I've Gotta Be Me'—all ego songs. She said, 'Whatever happened to songs like "I Love *You*" and "I Care About *You*" and "*You*'re Important"?' And Willie piped up and

said, 'You know, Paul Anka wrote "My Way" for Sinatra.'
And Mabel pulled herself up to all her five feet and said, 'Well,
he *shouldn't* have.' I'll never forget that."

Sam Hamilton fell ill with stomach cancer in the early 1960s
and was no longer able to accompany Mabel. He returned to
his home in Indiana where he died a few years later. Mabel felt
this loss deeply. Sam hadn't been the greatest piano player in
the world, but he had been intensely loyal, and always there.
"He was a very nice guy," says Will Craik, "never a brilliant
pianist but a very good accompanist, and Mabel always insisted
there was a great deal of difference between somebody who
was a good accompanist as compared to just a good piano
player, and she knew whereof she spoke." In her own way
Mabel had also supported Sam, often going to dinner at Goldie's
on Lexington Avenue where Sam played for the supper crowd
before joining Mabel wherever she happened to be appearing.
For a time, Mabel was without a regular accompanist, but since
she was also without regular employment, she simply got
whomever she could to accompany her when she did perform.
There was never a shortage of pianists who were eager to play
for her, among them Jimmy Lyon, whose regular gig at the
time was at the Blue Angel, where he worked with Bart Howard. It was Lyon who accompanied her at her Town Hall Concert with Bobby Short.

George Wein, creator of the Newport Jazz Festival, organized the concert. A longtime friend of both Mabel's and
Bobby's, he had often thought of pairing them in an evening
of nostalgia, and when he acted on his idea he did it in a big
way. Not only did he arrange for them to sing at Town Hall,
he also arranged for Atlantic to record the event and for society
columnist Rex Reed to write the liner notes.

Mabel and Jimmy Lyon rehearsed for weeks before the
concert, not only because Lyon was unaccustomed to accompanying her but also because Mabel was terrified of the event.
She was not used to singing in large auditoriums and was worried that her voice would not be heard. Besides, more than

fifty years in show business had not rid her of stage fright. Says Will Craik, "We used to kid her that she always suffered for exactly seventy-two hours before a big concert." Then, of course, she had to decide what sort of gown to wear and sew it, and what color stole to wear, and sew that. And when it rained the night of the concert, she worried about getting her shoes wet.

"It rained that night," wrote Reed, remembering the memorable evening of May 19, 1968, "and the headlights of the Bentleys and the chauffeured limousines that tied up the traffic in front of Town Hall made lavender reflections in the asphalt of the jungle night. Everything had changed, yet nothing had changed at all. A new generation had discovered them all over again through the deliciousness of their songs. The rich and the famous came, pausing briefly to observe the Andy Warhol superstars smiling brokenly for the flashbulbs. Youthful college kids came, only recently converted to the ageless cult of Mercer-Short worshippers. Women you used to read about in Cholly Knickerbocker's columns came, fading film stars in their last forty pounds of unhocked jewels and aging millionaires who never wander west of Fifth Avenue anymore except to sail for Europe came. And suddenly, in the burnished hush of the concert hall, so jammed that pop society and old guard duennas crowded together onstage like Brueghel paintings, Mabel and Bobby were there, blossoming in the artificial footlights like sunflowers nourished by neon."[5]

Bobby Short sang first. His was a selection of songs by Cole Porter, Jerome Kern, Cy Coleman, and others, all done in his ultracharming way: Porter's "I'm Throwing a Ball Tonight," "That Black and White Baby of Mine," "Looking at You," and "I Love You (Samantha)," Coleman's "When in Rome" and "I've Got Your Number," Jerome Kern's and Dorothy Fields's "Bojangles of Harlem," Billy Strayhorn's and Duke Ellington's "Something to Live For." He displayed all the sparkling chic for which he was famous, and some observers believed there was a fresh, unhackneyed manner in his singing

143

and suggested that it might have been because he knew how special it was to sing on the same program as Mabel Mercer, whom he had first heard in 1945 and who'd strongly influenced him.

After intermission, Mabel appeared onstage. The entire crowd rose to acclaim her, and with a nod she stepped to the high-backed armchair that had been placed there for her, folded her hands in her lap, and began to sing. Two microphones bowed gracefully to her from either side. Even so, she was difficult to hear. Her "graceful parlando" melted into singing on occasion, and if there was a slight quaver in her voice, it seemed to underscore her dramatic intent. She sang Porter's "All of You," Cy Coleman's "Isn't He Adorable," "Bad Is for Other People," "You Should See Yourself," and "Sweet Talk," as well as other songs from her repertoire.

At the finale, Mabel and Bobby sang together—Paul Simon's "The 59th Street Bridge Song" and Cy Coleman's "Here's to Us." Wrote Kevin Kelly, drama critic for the *Boston Globe*, "In the odd blending of their voices, and their distinctly separate styles, they were nothing less than wonderful."[6]

Congratulatory telegrams and telephone calls poured in. People from across the country wrote Mabel notes. The double album of the concert issued by Atlantic was nominated for a Grammy award. Mabel enjoyed it all, and when George Wein and Bobby Short suggested a return engagement the following year, Mabel acceded, although she realized she faced another period of worry and fright. She had no way of knowing that she would shortly have a lot more serious matters to worry about.

Harry's health was the most serious. First, he broke his leg. "We were in the city," says Will Craik, "on the way to Goldie's one night. We'd been to a cocktail party on 59th Street and were walking over to Goldie's, which was about five or six blocks, and Harry tripped on a curb and fell, and by the time we got to Goldie's his ankle was swollen up like a balloon. From there, we went to the hospital."

Harry recuperated at the farm in Red Rock, but hardly had the leg healed before he developed phlebitis. In between engagements, which were not frequent during the spring and summer of 1968, Mabel attended to him. Then, she herself was hospitalized at the nearby Berkshire Medical Center with diverticulitis. Fortunately, it was not serious; she was soon released with the warning that she would have to watch what she ate. "She used to be a great cook," says Will Craik, "but she didn't do much cooking after that. She lost quite a bit of weight, and was very proud of it."

She returned for a short engagement at Downstairs at the Upstairs in November (at the time, Joan Rivers was the regular attraction there), and signed a contract for a month's engagement at the Cafe Carlyle at Madison Avenue at 76th Street the next January. Then Harry had a heart attack.

For her engagement at the Cafe Carlyle, an intimate room which John S. Wilson of *The New York Times* said would be ideal for Mabel "if the waiters could be silenced,"[7] Mabel had as her accompanist Buddy Barnes, who would remain with her for several years. "I knew Buddy Barnes when he was playing in Nantucket every summer," says Peter Conway. "I had a house there for a number of years, and Mabel performed with Buddy at a benefit there in the summer of 1968. As a matter of fact, Leslie Crosley, another old accompanist of Mabel's—before Bart Howard and Sam Hamilton—played out his last years in Nantucket. Anyway, Buddy was certainly not getting far as a singing pianist and was getting louder and more and more of a foot-stomper, and getting really rotten, I thought. I don't know how the introduction happened, but he was introduced to Mabel and all of a sudden he became very grand again—you know, 'I'm Mabel Mercer's accompanist now.'"

In February 1969, Mabel was honored at the Museum of the City of New York on upper Fifth Avenue by the Friends of the Museum's Theater and Music Collection. The occasion was her presentation to the museum's collection of the Lisa

Rhana study of the three faces of Mabel. (Rhana also did a charcoal drawing of Mabel in 1968 which was the focal point of an exhibition staged to accompany the publication of *Cole Porter* by Robert Kimball and Brendan Gill.) Mabel's presentation was then followed by a Sunday afternoon concert in the museum's auditorium and Mabel, accompanied by Buddy Barnes, chose not to present a fixed program but instead to select spontaneously from her repertoire. Given that she and Barnes had not been working together long, her choosing to do a spontaneous program indicates her trust in him. Says Bart Howard, "Buddy's crazy [but] I think he might have been Mabel's best accompanist."

Three months later, Mabel and Bobby Short returned to Town Hall for a second concert, which *Variety* called "a recurring rite of spring." Continued the review: "Miss Mercer's followers constitute a fiercely devoted cult who cherish her guilelessness, emotional power and phrasing gifts. But to the uninitiated the fuss remains a puzzlement. The voice is gone and her approach becomes monotonous over an hour's stretch. But she can communicate feeling with sincerity, and there are no clinkers in her catalog. A high spot was a delightfully revealing rendition of Joni Mitchell's 'Both Sides Now.' "[8] This concert was also recorded and the resulting album called *The Realm of Mercer and Short*.

Peter Spivak and his wife attended that concert, in front-row seats. "You know how the applause seems to cascade toward one when one is in that location," he recalls. "Well, when Mabel Mercer came on stage, there was more than a cascade. There was a tumultuous cheer and the applause of the transfixed and transported. Of course, standing ovations were the rule for Mabel at the beginning and at the end of the concert.

"Afterward, we all went to Bobby's apartment for a party. In Bobby's living room there was a couch arrangement which Mabel found instantly, and people began coming over to talk to her. As the evening drew on, Lynne Redgrave and her husband and I ended up sitting with Mabel, and Mabel began talking about the Prince of Wales, Bricktop, and Paris, and for us who listened to her time seemed to stand still."[9]

For Mabel, these concerts and albums were a fitting cap on a decade during which she had experienced the vagaries of public taste more than she had cared to. She was delighted that she was back in vogue.

CHAPTER

VII

MABEL BACK IN FASHION

A PECULIAR THING happened in the early 1970s: intimate cabaret singing came back into style. According to some, among the reasons for this phenomenon are the decline of rock 'n' roll into self-indulgence and amateurism and a yearning on the part of listeners for professionalism and craft. It would seem as though the era of huge concert "happenings" had exhausted itself, and that popular taste now sought out more musical experiences, to be enjoyed with just a few other people. There were a few younger performers who plied the intimate supper-club genre of entertaining, among them Ronny Whyte; but in the main it was the veteran performers in the intimate style who had the professionalism and craft to meet the new demand. It is not coincidental that toward the end of the Sixties such older performers as Maxine Sullivan, who had preceded Mabel Mercer at the Le Ruban Bleu in 1938, Hazel Scott (ten years Sullivan's junior but a performer since the age of sixteen), and of course Mabel Mercer began to enjoy a resurgence of popularity. By the early Seventies, Nellie Lutcher, Anita O'Day, Sarah Vaughan, Sylvia Sims, and a host of others had either resumed their careers or suddenly found work much easier to come by.

In the 1970s, at last, even Bricktop was welcomed by New York. She had closed her club in Rome around 1965 but had stayed on in the city she had come to love. In the middle 1960s she had spent a few years in Chicago caring for her sister Blonzetta, who subsequently died, and then had gone to California for several months before returning to Rome. But after two more years in Rome, she had decided, "If I was going to just live and not run a business anywhere, I figured I might as well return to the United States." She arrived in New York on December 29, 1970.[1]

Not long afterward, Bricktop made her first and only recording, *So Long, Baby* with Cy Coleman, and for nearly a decade worked as steadily as her health would allow at Huntington Hartford's club on East 56th Street, at Soerabaja on East 74th Street, at "21," at clubs in Chicago, and at the Playboy Club in London, each time informing her employers exactly what she required and exactly how her "clients," as she still called them, were to be treated. She didn't want them to have to pay for their drinks each time they ordered a round, for example, and she wanted to be able to buy a round of drinks for a table of her listeners without being presented with a tab on the spot. She wanted to entertain when she felt the time was right, not on a set schedule. She later remarked that some club owners and managers appreciated the advice, not having had much experience with the way things were done in the golden age of nightclubs.

When Mabel Mercer and Buddy Barnes began their first engagement at the St. Regis Hotel in the spring of 1972, Mabel also had to give the managers a few pointers. "They wanted me to start my first show at nine or nine-thirty," she told

Whitney Balliett that November, "and I told them that was too early. Much too early for my people. So I start around ten, and then what did they do at first but close the doors of the room at ten sharp and keep the people waiting outside until the second show began! 'Here, what's this?' I told them. 'You can't do that. These people rush away from their coffee to get here on time and find the doors shut in their faces.' So we've changed all that. They still close the doors, but they bring the late-comers in the back way."[2]

Once she'd set the people at the St. Regis straight about such things, Mabel enjoyed her engagement there immensely. So did Buddy Barnes. Says Bart Howard, "When he and Mabel went to work at the St. Regis, he took a suite and filled it full of flowers. This was very expensive—he must have spent every damn dime he made, and more." When the St. Regis invited them to return in September, both were eager to do so.

In the meantime, Mabel was invited to tape a Public Broadcasting Service special in South Carolina with Bobby Short. The special, which aired in November 1972, was shot in a studio decorated to resemble a luxurious penthouse drawing room. Mabel reminisced about the Paris years, and she and Short sang a medley of Cole Porter songs. Mabel sang "Just One of Those Things," and Bart Howard, who was there, repeated the word "Amen" in a camera close-up. Buddy Barnes gave her fine accompaniment. Says Howard, "While we were there Buddy tended to her like she was a baby. He never stopped watching to see that she was okay." Then suddenly, not long before she and Buddy were due to open at the St. Regis in the fall, Mabel learned that she would have to find another accompanist.

According to Peter Conway, "There was some wealthy woman, considerably older than he, and he decided it was time to get married. He just up and got married and off they went to Paris for their honeymoon, and he played there for a good six months or so. He just told Mabel he couldn't accompany her and I was quite annoyed with him. I thought, 'Here she's given you the chance of your lifetime to get out of this rut you're in, and this is how you treat her.' "

Until that time, Barnes had been "her favorite accompanist, by a long shot," recalls Will Craik. "He was a brilliant pianist and Mabel loved him when he was sober and steady. But he was not the most reliable. She was supposed to open at the St. Regis and he had promised her he would open with her there. But she called him—or Harry did, because she didn't like to handle business details—and he couldn't do it. He let her down on that one."

Mabel had three weeks to find another accompanist and rehearse with him before she opened at the St. Regis. Fortunately for her, the Blue Angel had folded and Jimmy Lyon was available. He had accompanied her on occasion before, but he had never been her regular accompanist. His widow, Christine, recalls, "They rehearsed for days at her place because he was overwhelmed with the material—he just didn't think he could do it. But they got it done." Not only was Mabel's second engagement at the St. Regis successful, but her collaboration with Jimmy Lyon was as well.

"She had easily a thousand songs," says Christine Lyon. "He was amazed at her memory—he would always talk about her memory. Sometimes she'd pull out something that she hadn't sung for years, which he felt was wrong because he loved getting down to rehearsing a piece of work for many hours so that they both knew it well. There were times when she would be anxious to do a song, even though she wasn't ready, and there would be a little bit of a friendly battle there, back and forth. They were good together, but he thought it was best for her to do the things that were right at her fingertips, because she did them so well."

During that engagement at the St. Regis, Mabel stayed at the hotel and Harry Beard joined her, for she needed him to handle the publicity she was receiving that fall. Not only did the PBS special air in November, but Whitney Balliett interviewed her for an article in *The New Yorker*, and to top it off, she made another rare television appearance, this time on the *Dick Cavett Show*. Balliett accompanied her and Harry to the taping, and described a typical example of the way they related to each other. She was nervous, and Beard remarked that it had taken seventy-two hours to prepare her. "She's like a child who has to go to the hospital. I finally told her if she wasn't careful she'd be all right. But she's so natural and offhand-seeming she can't go wrong. Mabel has walked alone. She has never deviated from what she knew had to be done. It has never been a question of money or vogue." After the taping of the show, Mabel left the studio to find a crowd of autograph seekers. Writing slowly, she signed her name a dozen times before a burly ABC policeman ushered her to a car. Inside the car, Mabel remarked that it was the first time she had ever been besieged by autograph seekers. "You're a living legend, Mabel," said Harry. "Don't say that, Harry," she replied. "It makes me nervous."[3]

Mabel was not really comfortable with such publicity, and never had been. She was more uncomfortable now because she realized she was getting on and was far more liable to do something embarrassing, like forgetting lyrics. Such lapses had begun to occur with some frequency by the early 1970s. The *Variety* review of her first engagement at the St. Regis mentioned that Buddy Barnes had to prompt her on occasion. Christine Lyon recalls, "Jimmy would whisper the lyrics to her, and the audience would notice it and they would giggle; it was cute." Mabel did not find it cute; she found it distressing. But she was in no position to retire. She still had to "sing for her supper." She would have preferred staying at the farm in Red Rock, and particularly at that time, if she'd had the choice that is exactly where she would have been, protecting her interests.

By then, Harry Beard had developed Parkinson's disease and had moved up to the farm, primarily, according to Will Craik, because he was embarrassed to be seen in a palsied condition. Given the choice, he would not have lived full-time with the field mice, which touched off one of the biggest arguments he and Mabel ever had.

Craik recalls, "One night we were up there and I was upstairs and I heard this violent row downstairs—Mabel never raised her voice, but Harry was cursing and swearing. I went downstairs, and Mabel was practically doubled over laughing, but Harry—I've never seen him so mad, I thought he was going to have apoplexy. This little field mouse had crawled into his bed with him, and nothing would do but for him to leave immediately. He was going to take the car and leave—'I'm going back to the city where they don't have this———!' And finally, Mabel said, 'No, you are not going to take the car in for that.' He said, 'Well, I'm not going back in that room.'

"Mabel had built a bedroom for herself with an adjoining bath downstairs so she wouldn't have to crawl upstairs, so Harry appropriated that room. But the next morning they were back upstairs. At breakfast he was still fuming about it—'Damn it, if you kept this house in proper order . . .' It was all her fault that the mouse had crawled into bed with him, because of her sloppy housekeeping. But of course that wasn't true; if the place had been broom clean, they still would have had mice. And she just finally looked at him and said, 'Just keep it up, and you're going to wake up tomorrow and neither Willie nor I is going to be here. I don't care where you go. You can get out.' Boy, that stopped him cold in his tracks. He never thought he'd hear this from Mabel."

In the thirty years he knew Mabel, Craik can recall only three times when she was angry—the time when Harry disappeared with the woman they'd met on their trip to California in 1960, the time the mouse climbed into bed with Harry, and the time a good friend of hers tried to move in on Harry.

This relationship had begun during a period when Harry was staying at the farm. Mabel would like to have stayed there with him, but since she was working fairly steadily, she could not be there to care for him and thus was at first grateful when a neighbor volunteered to do so. As time went on, Harry and the neighbor lady developed an exceptionally close friendship, and, initially, Mabel regarded the situation with characteristic humor. "We called the woman 'the Night Nurse,' " says Will Craik.

Since Harry was a great womanizer, not even Parkinson's

disease slowed him down. "He still traveled up to Rochester on the train to see his 'specialist,' " says Will Craik, who by then was suffering from ill health himself and spending a great deal of time in Red Rock. "Mabel would get exasperated and say, 'What Mr. Beard doesn't realize is that when you get to a certain age some things are not as important as they used to be, they just *aren't*.' But she wasn't prepared to lose Harry."

For his part, Harry was not likely to risk losing Mabel, and no doubt Mabel knew that. They had been together for many, many years and had come to depend on one another. Harry's womanizing was . . . Harry. The "Night Nurse," however, was not as intimately acquainted with Harry's character as Mabel was, and assumed more than she ought to have. Says Craik, "One of my favorite stories about Mabel is the time we were walking on Main Street in Chatham. The whole community was buzzing with this rumor that Mrs. X was going to divorce her husband and marry Harry. Of course there was nothing to it, but it didn't contribute to Mabel's peace of mind, let's put it that way. So we were walking down Main Street when this woman comes up. She said, 'Oh, Miss Mercer, I'm so happy to hear the news. I think it's just wonderful.' Mabel said, 'And what news is that?' She said, 'Oh, I'm so pleased that when Mrs. X gets her divorce she's going to marry your manager, Mr. Beard.' Mabel never batted an eye. She just looked at her and said, 'No, dear, I could never allow *that* to happen. Mrs. X is a *friend* of mine.' I broke up, I just couldn't hold it in; I had to walk away.

"But Mabel put up with it. I'm not sure how long she would have continued to do so. Fortunately, it didn't last long."

Apparently, Mrs. X realized that Harry was not going to leave Mabel and marry her, and not wanting to lose Mabel's friendship, she called on Mabel and informed her that she hadn't known the real relationship between Harry and Mabel. Will Craik remembers, "One night my telephone rang. It was Mabel, and she was really annoyed. She said, 'I have just heard the cock-and-bull story of all time.' I said, 'What was that, dear?'

And she said, 'The Night Nurse was over here, and she told me she *never knew* Harry and I were lovers.' She said, 'Do you believe that, dear?' I said, 'I'll sell you a bridge I know about.' She said, 'What does she take me for, some kind of fool?' She was furious, but we talked for a while and she simmered down. It was one of the few times I ever knew Mabel to be angry."

As much as she wanted to be at home on the farm in Red Rock, Mabel enjoyed the fact that she had found a new "home" at the St. Regis and some of the old sense of belonging in the world of New York night life. In the fall of 1974, the New York *Daily News* ran an article on her and Bricktop, who was appearing at Soerabaja at the time, and the two veteran entertainers no doubt enjoyed appearing on the same page again. They talked on the telephone frequently, and on occasion met at some club or other, although Bricky, due to both age (she was then eighty-one) and inclination, was less likely to go out except to perform. Columnist Jack O'Brian found them together at P.J.'s one night, reminiscing about Paris and Cole Porter and doing the "Shim Sham Shimmy" to his songs.

By this time, Donald Smith, a publicist who was a fan of Mabel's and who felt she needed his help, was doing publicity for Mabel. Harry Beard was no longer able to do it. His Parkinson's disease was so bad that he could barely write, although he could still handle the telephone. That really disturbed Mabel. "She was funny that way," says Will Craik. "When she got to know somebody and depended on them, she hated any interruptions in the routine. Harry was supposed to take care of the lights, Harry was supposed to take care of this and that. And when he could no longer do it, she was all upset about it. I always mowed the lawn, and then my legs went bad and I couldn't do it anymore. She said, 'Oh, what am I going to do?' She hated any drastic changes in her routine; she liked things to just go on as they had always been."

But age was taking its toll, not only on those around her but on Mabel herself. After Harry could no longer drive, Mabel took it upon herself to do more driving, although she had never been very good at it. Says Craik, "A lot of people wouldn't ride with her. Mabel only wanted half the road but she wanted the middle half. You'd go, 'Oh, what a beautiful tree over there,' and the next thing you knew you'd be right up against it. It got so I was the only one who would ride with her, even into Chatham to go shopping." Then one day Mabel was driving her 1967 Plymouth station wagon home after taking one of her cats to the veterinarian, and the cat was acting up in its box. She reached in to quiet the animal, and a front wheel went off the road. Struggling to get the wheel back on the road, she went far over into the opposite lane where a car was coming up fast from the other direction. To avoid the oncoming car, she swerved off the road into a field, and right into a fence. The whole passenger side of the car was pushed in, and it was difficult to even open the door. The car was completely out of alignment. The local garage estimated that it would cost a thousand dollars to repair, and Mabel didn't have that kind of money to spend on car repairs. Besides, the accident caused her to lose her nerve. "I had just built a little garage, too," Mabel said later, "and there it sits—full of Plymouth."

Fortunately, Mabel had friends to drive her—Will Craik, Adde Wallin-Beach, Muriel Finch. As the years passed, she came to depend on them more and more. Muriel now did much of the bookkeeping that Harry had done. Adde drove her wherever she wanted to go. Will did whatever he could, including driving her to church in Chatham. "Every Sunday, come hell or high water, she had to go to St. James. Nobody else could get down the road, but we had to try. Then they started having Mass at five-thirty Saturday night, and she would go to that so we wouldn't have to get up Sunday morning. She always used to say, 'It's so hard getting *you* up in the morning.' That was her alibi for going Saturday night, although I think she really liked it better herself." He made her laugh. She made him laugh. "She had a marvelous sense of humor. She was so dry and so witty at times. Right when you least expected it, she'd zing one right in there, and if you weren't listening it would go right over your head, and later when you'd think of it you'd laugh and laugh."

While her personal life seemed to be beset by change and readjustment, Mabel's professional life could not have been better. Of the St. Regis, she said, "I guess I would call this room my home base. I don't know if the management does, but I do. I like it here, and people who want to hear me always know where to find me." The management apparently had no complaints either, for in the spring of 1975 the St. Regis Roof was the setting for a gala seventy-fifth birthday party for her. In addition to Mabel Mercer buttons, which were handed out to the four hundred or so guests, and a huge cake, there was a ceremony where a plaque was unveiled, renaming the St. Regis Room the Mabel Mercer Room. There were, in fact, so many displays of affection that Mabel was heard to remark, "This is the kissiest party I've ever been to!"

Wrote Rex Reed, "It was sad that some of the biggest names who claim to have learned all they know from Mabel Mercer didn't show up. Frank Sinatra, Peggy Lee and Leontyne Price sent telegrams. Sarah Vaughan, who was scheduled to sing a birthday song for Mabel, was missing. But there was enough glamour and music for all. The mayor's office gave Mabel the key to the city. Leonard Bernstein acclaimed her 'the eternal guardian of elegance in the world of popular music.' Warren Beatty said, 'When you hear her sing, you know, she becomes your wife, mother, sister, mistress and accountant.' Sylvia Sims and Cy Coleman sang 'The Best Is Yet to Come.' Thelma Carpenter performed an old 1920s medley from *Blackbirds* to signal the year she first met Mabel, and Bobby Short deserted his own piano bench to sing Cole Porter standing up."

Continued Reed, "But the best part of the evening came when Mabel herself descended to the stage, sat on her Louis Quinze throne and sang. And when she sang the intelligence and imagination brought tears to the eyes of grown men. She knows everything worth knowing about the interpretation of lyrics. Her selection of material is faultless, the sound is that of a lonely cello behind a vocal line drawn with an emotional artistry unmatched by any other singer. The once fine soprano has grown parched with the years, but the impact is the same."[4]

To coincide with this birthday celebration, Atlantic issued a boxed set titled *A Tribute to Mabel Mercer on the Occasion of Her 75th Birthday*, consisting of four of the albums she made in the 1950s. Stanyan reissued an album she had made at approximately the same time for Decca. These two reissues, added to Atlantic's two-record set *The Art of Mabel Mercer*, and the two 2-record sets made at Town Hall with Bobby Short, made Mabel's entire recorded canon available, a remarkable circumstance for any performer but particularly so for Mabel, who had, as it was frequently pointed out, "never had a hit record."

In March 1975, Mabel made one of her rare trips away from New York to appear, with Jimmy Lyon, at John McNulty's Cafe Lafitte in Philadelphia—the first singer to be booked there for four weeks and the first to be booked for two shows nightly. While there she did a local television program called *The Mark of Jazz*. She appeared on television very rarely, and when she did she refused to watch herself, although she did keep a videotape of the Philadelphia program.

It remained an exciting time for Mabel. In May she was awarded an honorary doctorate by Berklee College of Music in Boston, a citation that seemed especially to gratify her, for she had not been able to pursue her formal education when she was young. Not only Will Craik and Harry Beard, but Harry's sister, Pearl Lemert, Alec Wilder, and Cy Coleman accompanied her to share in her happiness. That same year she was given the first annual Stereo Review Award of Merit.

In between award ceremonies, Mabel continued to work at the Mabel Mercer Room at the St. Regis.

Among her occasional accompanists was Richard Rodney Bennett, the British classical composer-turned-club singer and pianist. Peter Conway had introduced them. "After Sam's tragic death, Mabel and I saw each other occasionally, but whenever we did meet it was as if we were regular and good friends.

We'd do some 'catching up' for a few minutes, and the old, warm relationship would be the same as always.

"When Richard Rodney Bennett first came to America to teach at Peabody in Baltimore, I gave a party for him and asked primarily 'club' singers, as I knew that was one of his consuming musical passions then (he has since become a club singer and pianist himself, with several show albums to his credit). At any rate, he most especially wanted to meet Mabel, and of course I asked her. When she was unable to come on the appointed evening, she asked if she might take a rain check and come another time to meet him, which I was happy to arrange.

"She and her companion, Harry Beard, came to my apartment on a sweltering summer's day, but Mabel asked that I turn off the air conditioning, as she didn't like it. I had gotten some champagne for her, and the four of us—Mabel, Harry, Richard, and myself—plus my companion, Paul, spent a delightful afternoon. Mabel asked if she might roll her stockings down because of the heat—and she did! Richard sang a number of his club songs for her, and played, and as a result of all that Richard and Mabel became very good friends. I believe he accompanied her more than once at the St. Regis Hotel after she opened her Mabel Mercer Room there, and I think she was very instrumental in getting him started on the whole new career he now pursues."

At the St. Regis, Mabel added several new songs to her repertoire, among them Joe Raposo's "Being Green," which had gained its first popularity on TV's *Sesame Street*. Recalls Peter Spivak, "Next to my memory of Mabel at her concert at Town Hall with Bobby Short, and at Bobby's afterward, my favorite Mabel memory was when my son, who was then a toddler, was in the room when my wife and I were playing a Mabel Mercer record. When the song 'Being Green' came on, little Peter's identification was immediate, and I was present at the onset of his becoming a Mabel Mercer fan."

Perhaps her most often requested song at this time was

"Send in the Clowns," written by Stephen Sondheim. "Her version of 'Send in the Clowns' almost sums up her art," wrote London newspaper columnist Robert Cushman; "the recurring title-phrase is treated differently each time it comes round; it begins nonchalant and ends up fierce. She also insists, more firmly than any other singer, on this song as a waltz; a rhythm to which she is peculiarly sensitive."[5] Says Loonis McGlohon, who accompanied her often during the latter part of the 1970s, "She analyzed that song upside down before she did it. She didn't think that some singers ever understood what it was all about; I think she was the one who really discovered how to do that song." Many others agreed. Says Christine Lyon, widow of Jimmy Lyon, "I remember Sinatra telling my husband, Jimmy, that he never enjoyed the song until he heard her do it, until he sat up and listened to the words. Jimmy felt the same way. The timing—he was always floored with her flawless timing. He said it came from long years of singing, that it doesn't happen with two or three jobs. He used to say, 'You'd have to do what she does. You just can't get away with anything else. You can't think about going home and cleaning house or making dinner.' "

In the summer of 1977, Mabel returned to Europe for the first time since her hasty departure in 1938. The occasion was the opening of a new room, The Playmate Grille, at the London Playboy Club, and since Mabel had opened the first after-hours room at the Playboy Club in Chicago seventeen years earlier, it was somehow fitting that she help to inaugurate that intimate, supper-club room in London. Mabel agreed to the engagement because she wanted to see London, and Paris, one last time.

Bobby Short gave a bon voyage party for Mabel at his apartment in the Osborn on West 57th Street. When he asked Mabel whom she wanted him to invite, she suggested Alberta Hunter. Mabel had known Alberta since the Thirties, when Bricktop had introduced them at her club in Paris. Bricktop knew Hunter from her Chicago days before World War I when

Hunter, born in Memphis in 1895, achieved her first fame as a singer. Hunter was also a songwriter, and it was Bessie Smith's rendition of her song "Down Hearted Blues" that had propelled Smith to stardom in 1923.

As both a singer and a songwriter, Hunter was internationally famous until the late Forties, when her career began to wane. The death of her mother in New York in 1954 caused her to decide to help others who were suffering, and for a year she volunteered at the Hospital for Joint Diseases in Manhattan, winning recognition as Volunteer of the Year in 1956. In the meantime, she had decided to train as a practical nurse. Having quit school at age sixteen to go to Chicago to be a singer, she earned her high school equivalency diploma. Armed with that, she went to the YWCA school on West 137th Street in Manhattan to enroll in the nurse's training course offered there. The director of the program said she was too old, but Hunter begged and cajoled and finally the director gave in. She lopped twelve years off Hunter's age and enrolled her as a fifty-year-old student.

Hunter began her career as a practical nurse at Goldwater Hospital in May 1957 and spent twenty happy years there until she was involuntarily retired by the personnel office, according to whose records she had reached the age of seventy. During those years, she had lost touch with most of her contacts in the entertainment world, although in the 1960s she recorded two albums at the behest of Danish jazz critic Chris Albertson. She kept in touch with Bricktop and Mabel, however, and Mabel suggested that Bobby Short invite her to the bon voyage party because she hoped that Hunter, retired and with too much time on her hands, might be persuaded to come. Mabel warned Short that getting Alberta to come might take some persuading.

Short sent Hunter an engraved invitation. When she did not respond, he followed up with a formal reminder. When she still did not answer, Short sought help from Jimmy Daniels, singer and former owner of the club Bon Soir and a mutual friend of Alberta's and Mabel's. Daniels told Hunter she was going to the party if he had to drag her there. Hunter went, but she was not amusing and funny, as Mabel hoped she would be. On the contrary, she was very quiet. She did not even dress up.

Nevertheless, Charlie Bourgeois, an organizer of the Newport Jazz Festival, and Alec Wilder noticed her and introduced themselves. One chorus of "Down Hearted Blues" convinced them that she ought to be singing somewhere so that others could hear her. By the next day she had a job at Barney Josephson's Greenwich Village club, The Cookery. For the next seven years, until her death in 1984 at the age of eighty-nine, she sang at the club, recorded, and even composed the music for Robert Altman's film *Remember My Name*. Mabel, thus, was at least indirectly responsible for the most astonishing career resumption of the decade.[6]

"We crossed together on the *QE2*," says columnist Rex Reed. "Mabel and Jimmy Lyon were headed for London and they gave two concerts, I think, on the ship. We had an enormous storm at sea and everything on the boat was turned upside down, and the next morning every one of us on the ship was seasick except Mabel. She appeared in the dining room first thing bright and early, and she said, 'Oh, my dear, I've been up all night chasing my furniture, all over the room.' She could have taken care of the whole ship. She never missed a meal."

Harry Beard accompanied Mabel on that trip, the last that they would take together. Thin and frail, he nevertheless rose to the occasion, and no doubt Mabel was grateful for the opportunity to share her memories with him. Sadly, she found that her memories were really all she could get from that trip. "They went to Paris because she wanted to see it again," says Christine Lyon. "She could not believe the change—and was quite disappointed in it."

"When I went back to Paris, it was beautiful," Mabel said the following year. "But I went up to Montmartre—went up at nighttime—and it was like walking down 42nd Street, which is . . . I don't know. I couldn't live there again. I couldn't believe it, it all looked so different. All the ugly pictures—oversized, nude pictures of girls. . . . It's all so wrong."[7]

Mabel disappointed many people who questioned her about her trip in the hope of garnering information. She was especially close-mouthed about the British royal family. Recalls Loonis McGlohon, music director for WBTV in Charlotte, North Carolina, who got to know her shortly after her return, "Mabel was very secretive, very protective about her friendships with royalty. I saw her do an interview where she was asked about her friendship with the Queen Mother. I saw her, not bristle, but get tense. She said, 'The Queen Mother is a lovely lady.' So the interviewer said, 'I'm sure you know Queen Elizabeth.' Mabel said, 'I prefer not to talk about the royal family.' The only thing she told me about them was that the Duke or Duchess of Windsor, or maybe both, helped her get out of Paris, *told* her to get out of Paris. She told me she walked away and left everything in her apartment and never went back. I said, 'Never went back, Mabel?' She said, 'No.' I said, 'What happened?' She said, 'I'm sure the Germans confiscated everything I had.' I said, 'I can't imagine your not going to that address to see what was there.' It baffles me that she would walk away and close that door and never go back. But Mabel was like that."

Julius Monk, however, understands exactly how Mabel felt. "I went back in 1985 and I felt like a male version of Frances Skeffington. You can't look back. We weren't tourists, we lived there, it was our livelihood. It was like returning to IBM for a visit. I go to strange cities now—it's much wiser."

Mabel's engagement at the Playboy Club was highly successful. Says Christine Lyon, "The kids at Playboy—their first reaction was, 'What is *she* doing here?' But she won them over and they loved her." Tristram Powell, a producer-director at the BBC, noted the impact Mabel was making and arranged to tape her performances. The BBC televised them nightly for a week and subsequently Powell produced a sixty-minute program, "Miss Mercer at Mayfair," splicing performance footage with interviews.

The Playboy Club organization realized it had a winner in Mabel. A couple of years later, they invited her to the Bahamas to preside at the opening of the new Playboy Club there. Recalls Bart Howard, "She called me up one day and said that Playboy was opening a place in Nassau and wanted her to come down and would I go with her. We hadn't been to Nassau in all those years. I said, 'I'll have to have my dinner jacket let out, but I'll come,' and by God, we went! Of course, Nassau was something else—the British Colonial is now a Howard Johnson's. We didn't recognize the street. Cy Coleman was also along on that trip—he had written the theme song for the Bunnies."

Coincidentally, around this time the Playboy Club organization also sought out Bricktop. In 1978, she returned to London to perform at the club there. Afterward, she and Mabel commiserated about the sad inevitability of change.

Back in the United States, Mabel did a show for National Public Radio, part of a series called *American Popular Song* co-hosted by Alec Wilder and Loonis McGlohon. "Alec wanted Mabel to do one of the shows, so she did, and I got to know her well then," says McGlohon, "although I had met her earlier, through Alec, and heard her at Downstairs at the Upstairs and other places.

"I first heard her, I guess, in the late Forties or early Fifties," McGlohon continues. "I'd heard that she was a legend, and I went and I really didn't like what I saw. I stayed through two shows and the vice president of the TV station where I was working heard her, and he suggested we go see her. I said, 'Great, because I don't know what all the fuss is about. I've heard her records and I don't like them.' I didn't like the first show, but we stayed for the second show, and then I saw, gradually I saw, what was happening. The power of communication was absolutely unmatched—nobody could interpret a song like she could. It is something that is difficult to explain in words, I'm afraid it was a visual thing."

Mabel and McGlohon, whose mellifluous name must have attracted her immediately, not only became good friends but later also became professional collaborators.

By the fall of 1977, Mabel's comparatively long (by the standards of the day) engagement at the St. Regis had ended. She went next to Cleo, across from Lincoln Center, followed by her usual coterie of longtime fans, and, as Loonis McGlohon recalls, she was sought out by their sons and daughters as well.

"It was always amazing to me how reverent people were when they approached her. They never, for example, as they did with other celebrities, walked up and put a paper down in the soup bowl and said, 'Sign this, please.' They never did that with Mabel. If they touched her it was just on the hand, or very gently on the arm. Never any pulling or grabbing, or putting an arm around her. It was almost like touching someone royal. And I've seen them just gently touch her on the arm and say, 'Miss Mercer, I just want to say I love you, Miss Mercer.' One night at Cleo's my wife and I were sitting there with her and a young couple from Connecticut came over. They were in their twenties and they said, 'Our parents told us that we had to come to hear you and that you sang a song when they were in love and they came to see you and how much a part of their life you are, and now we see what they meant. Tonight was very special because we felt like you were singing something for us.' And it pleased Mabel when she saw people holding hands or exchanging a look. She was very observant about what was going on in the audience. When people came up and told her how she had touched them, she would say, 'How can they like this croaking sound I make?' But inside I think she knew."

Samuel V. K. Willson recalls with some pride that he introduced a young friend of his to Mabel when she was appearing at the St. Regis: "He had never heard her in person and didn't think very much of her records. But he was certainly glad to have a chance to hear—experience—this goddess I so revered. In her big chair, with the pinpoint spot, and the long scarf, she was magical! Not many people were in the small room, but I remember that Rex Reed was there, mesmerized like the rest of us. When Mabel finished, my friend and I left—and came across her standing alone in the lobby, catching her breath. I told her that I'd been a fan of hers since my late Forties college days and introduced my young friend, who was duly awestruck. She was chuckly and charming as I gushed, and gracious to my friend and appreciative of our coming to hear the 'old lady trying to sing.' So now, of course, it's my young friend who gives Mabel Mercer records as Christmas gifts, and who feels wounded when his friends can't understand what he sees in her."[8]

As much as she enjoyed young people, it is perhaps sad that Mabel never had any children. Mabel rarely discussed the matter, although in early 1978, during an interview in New York with a reporter from the *San Francisco Examiner and Chronicle*, she responded to the question, 'If you had your life to live over . . . ?' with, "Oh, I suppose there are many things, many mistakes. I should have been a woman with about six children. I like people. I like young people too. They look upon me as a sweet old grandmother. So many of them say to me, 'Can I hug you?' And I say, 'Go ahead.' "[9]

But not having children was something that Mabel had accepted long before, and as she had grown older she had begun to regard young children with a bit of suspicion. "Her animals were like her children," says Will Craik. "As for real children: I think it was W. C. Fields who, when asked if he liked children, said, 'Yes, if they're properly cooked.' Mabel liked children, but *only* after breakfast. She could not take them before breakfast. I remember one Fourth of July weekend. My sister was going someplace further north; she had three children and she stopped off to see me at Mabel's, to say hello. This was sometime in the Sixties. The pianist Cy Walter and his wife and their three children were up. So there were six children, and they just adored Mabel, they really did. But she would come down in the morning, and they would all be around her, you know, and she would say, 'Out! Not till after breakfast!' Oh, no, not until she'd had her cup of tea.

"Of course, for Mabel that could take half the morning. It was the most amazing thing. She'd start making tea for herself. She made it by the potful, and she'd pour herself a cup of tea. And then something would divert her attention—something she'd meant to take care of and hadn't, or the phone would ring, or she'd decide to go over and pet the cat or let the cat out or feed the dog. By then the tea would be too cold—it had to be *hot*—and she'd go out and pour it on the ground. It took I don't know how long before she got a good, hot cup of tea inside her."

Mabel returned to San Francisco in January 1978, this time to perform at Richard Wasson's Mocambo for four weeks. Her old friend George Cory helped to arrange it. He and Douglass Cross had moved to San Francisco, where Cross had family property, about ten years earlier. Sadly, Douglass Cross had died about five years before, and George Cory would die soon after Mabel's trip to San Francisco. Bob Adams, Cross's former colleague at WNYC, was then an announcer at WNCN, and at Cory's request he traveled to Red Rock to do a taped interview with Mabel for use during her appearance on the West Coast.

Mabel traveled to San Francisco by train, commenting, "At my age, what's the hurry?" To celebrate her seventy-eighth birthday, the BBC sent a crew from London to film one of her performances. She spent part of her birthday autographing her albums at a nearby record store. At her performance that evening, her show was interrupted by tumultuous applause several times, periodic cascades of flowers, and a singing telegram. California Secretary of State March Fong Eu showed up with a proclamation honoring her. But Mabel really showed what she was made of when she performed at the huge Dorothy Chandler Pavilion in Los Angeles that same year. Jimmy Lyon accompanied her. "He was so proud of that," says his widow, Christine. "Jimmy was very much a little boy when it came to things like that. He could not believe he actually did it—that tremendous stage."

To outside observers Mabel seemed unstoppable, but she herself was beginning to wonder how long she could continue. "She started getting vertigo," says Christine Lyon. "She had dizzy spells, and she decided it was time to stop." There was no farewell performance, no gala retirement party. Mabel just went up to the farm in Red Rock for a rest that lasted about three years. "People kept questioning Jimmy about when she was coming back," says Lyon, "about whether or not she would consider coming back."

Mabel would have liked nothing better than to return to work, but she knew that was not possible. Recalls Will Craik, "She'd say, 'I can't put one foot in front of the other without popping over. The room is just going around me.' The doctors couldn't seem to find out what was causing it—they thought maybe it had to do with the inner ear, Nureyev's syndrome or something. She kept complaining about it. Also, her arthritis got worse, and the angina. And she had diverticulitis. When we were in the city she had gone to the famous/infamous doctor that they called Dr. Feelgood. His license got suspended. He was pumping people full of amphetamines. She swore by him, thought he was absolutely marvelous. She didn't understand what he was doing and was furious when he got into trouble. She *wouldn't* believe he had done anything wrong. Of course, when we got up here, she didn't have him, but she would still send down to the city and get pills from her drugstore."

Mabel kept in touch with what was going on in New York by continuing to invite as many people as she could to the farm. Says Allen Carter, "She would space them out: 'Are you available this coming weekend? Fine, because no one is coming up.' Or, 'One other person is coming up and you would mix well. Come up.' But her guests were primarily her younger friends. Those of her own era were also in poor health, and losing touch. Julius Monk recalls, "The last time I spoke to Mabel I called because I'd gone to the hospital to see Bricky after her heart attack. Mabel didn't know about it, and Bricky asked me to call Jimmy Daniels and Mabel, which I did. It is so strange—we were very close, and a clique through those glorious, gala, turbulent years of the Thirties in Paris."

Bricktop continued to perform for a couple of years after her heart attack, primarily in Chicago. Her last engagement was in New York at "21" with Hugh Shannon. She retired in 1979 because of debilitating arthritis and anemia.

Although he was himself in poor health, Alec Wilder continued to visit Mabel often in the country. He loved the farm nearly as much as she did, and among the dozens of songs he wrote for her that was never even copyrighted was one called "Up the Hill in Red Rock." "He owed her a great debt," says Loonis McGlohon, "because he said that of all the people he knew she did his songs best. I heard him say over and over, 'There's an aura of goodness about this lady. When you walk into a room where Mabel is, you see this aura around her. There's so much goodness.' "

Wilder died in December 1980. Says McGlohon, "After Alec died, Mabel told me, 'Alec brought me a tree. He planted a tree and said it was a walnut tree. It didn't bear for about three or four years, and as a matter of fact it was not long before he died that it began to bear. And I've never told him it was a hickory nut, that he'd bought the wrong tree. I think he would have been very hurt.' "

In 1981, McGlohon asked Mabel to reminisce about Wilder for a radio program he was producing. Mabel sighed, "Alec, I loved him dearly, because he was a great friend and he was such a sensitive man. He used to come and stay for a couple of days at a time at the farm, and one time he came up and he was rather dry in periods of writing—you know, all creative artists go through that—and a few days up there cured it. But he used to wander out in the fields and through the trees and everything. His room was under the roof, you know. It was a small room and I had the roof opened up and put a great big picture window in it, and I said, 'This is for you, so when you come you can sit here and write and look out at the trees.' Unfortunately, he passed on before it happened. But he's there, I'm sure.' "[10]

MABEL'S
LAST YEARS

WHILE MABEL was no longer performing, she had not given up singing. At the urging of Loonis McGlohon, she recorded for Audiophile some of the best examples of her art ever released. Several of the songs she learned especially for the sessions. McGlohon accompanied her, his work exquisitely perceptive of her phrasing and mood; according to one critic, it was his finest playing on record to date.[1] The set, called appropriately *Echoes of My Life* and released in celebration of Mabel's eightieth birthday, was a fitting testament to her half-century-plus as a singer.

On Monday, January 5, 1981, the Whitney Museum of American Art in New York City honored Mabel with a show called "An American Cabaret." The $150-a-person, black-tie evening (wrote columnist Rex Reed, "All the Missys and Chessys and Buffys and Muffys were there—enough swells to fill the society pages for months") was a benefit for the Whitney and its Composers' Showcase, and it was tantamount to a reunion for those who had composed and performed for supper clubs, including Bricktop and Buddy Barnes, Ronny Whyte, Cy Coleman, and Sylvia Sims. But Mabel was the guest of honor. Bart Howard sang "It Was Worth It" to her. Ronny Whyte dedicated and sang to Mabel an original composition about the great old days of New York night life, titled "Let Me Show You My New York," and Sammy Cahn wrote special lyrics to "It's Been a Long, Long Time." Mabel received awards and plaques from ASCAP and the American Theater Wing. And as Mabel mounted the stage to sing herself, Rex Reed overheard one ringsider say, "Look at the aristocracy in that face." "She should be knighted," said somebody else."[2] For Mabel, who had not performed for three years, it was a wonderful evening, and one that caused her to reconsider her retirement.

"She really missed singing," says Ronny Whyte, who saw Mabel frequently. "I did a series of concerts in Spencertown (which is near Chatham) in May and June of 1981. We called it 'The American Popular Song Book' and we dedicated the series to Alec Wilder and to Mabel. Mabel came to every one of the concerts. After each one Judy Juhring, a good friend whom I often visited and who was Mabel's neighbor, had a reception, and after the last three, Mabel sang with me at Judy's. We just sort of all sat around and jammed with whoever had been the artist, and Mabel would start singing. Everyone would say, 'Mabel, Mabel, sing a song,' and so she'd sing three or four songs. In fact, one day she must have done almost an hour, and she really loved it. She'd say, 'Oh, no, no one wants to hear me,' but she really missed singing."

In fact, it was only now that Mabel would consent to singing offstage, for since she had worked with Bricktop it had been her hard-and-fast rule not to sing unless she was paid for it. Singing was her profession. Says Will Craik, "Of course she used to rehearse up here on weekends—'ad nauseam,' I used to tell her. She was a perfectionist; she would go over and over and over a phrase until she got it exactly the way she wanted it—exactly. But she never played for herself, and she never got up and sang at parties. 'This is what I do for a living.' This was tantamount to asking a doctor at a party to take out your tonsils."

Recalls Adde Wallin-Beach, "In the garden sometimes when we worked in the earth—a fellow once called it dirt and she said, 'Dirt is what you have on your clothes when you get down on the floor. That's God's earth'—she'd hum, she'd sing. When my great-great-grandchild, Jennifer, was born, Mabel sat in a rocking chair and held her. She said, 'I've never seen a baby this small before.' Anne Francine [the singer] was there and she said, 'Mabel, sing one of your songs to the baby,' so she did. But she didn't often do that. Sometimes a record would be on, and we'd all start humming to it, and she'd join in, but if we all dropped out she'd say, 'Oh, I don't like that.'

"She hated listening to her own records. One day not too many years ago we were in Hudson shopping and we ate in a little place called the Neptune on Warren Street. Right across the way was a gift shop, so we went in. As soon as we walked in the door we heard one of her records, and I said, 'Oh, my Lord,' and Mabel said, 'Oh, no.' We didn't say anything to the chap who owned the store. He said, 'Do you mind if I leave that on? She's one of my favorite people.' He didn't really look at us. So we browsed around. Finally the record ended, and she said, 'Thank the Lord for that.' It made her uneasy. The clerk turned and said, 'Don't you like it?' and then he looked at her and sort of stopped and said, 'Do I know you?' I couldn't bear it another moment. I said, 'This is Mabel Mercer.' "

In June 1981, Mabel attended a tribute to Cole Porter on the ninetieth anniversary of his birth, appearing for the first time in public with her naturally gray hair. In the opinion of Joe Carstairs, it was about time. "She always looked slightly matronly, and when she got older it seemed silly to me that she continued to dye her hair. I used to say, 'Mabel, why don't you let your hair get white?' But she wouldn't. She always made it dark, you know." She also straightened it. Recalls Craik, "Right up until the last few years she dyed it very black, and used to do it with copious amounts of vaseline and one of those old curling irons you heat on the stove." The reason for the change probably had less to do with vanity than with practicality—Mabel's severe arthritis made it difficult for her to perform the physical motions of dyeing and straightening her hair. She was no longer able to work very much in her garden either, for bending down was too painful. She worried far more about neglecting her garden than about neglecting herself.

"She was slowing down," says Adde Wallin-Beach. "We'd go into town food shopping, and I'd go down one aisle and she'd go up another, and I'd say 'I'll meet you at the checkout.' And I'd see her sitting on a ledge, waiting for me, and then I began to realize that she was tiring, that she was not feeling well."

Still, she made an effort to see old friends, particularly those who believed that something had gone out of New York night life with Mabel's departure. By this time Bart Howard and his friend, Bud, were living in the country, too. Howard recalls, "One day the telephone rang and I heard this voice say, 'Bart?' And I said, 'Yes, Hermione [Gingold],' because she's the only person with a voice like that. She said, 'Where is everybody?' And I said, 'Who do you mean?' And she said, 'Oh . . . Mabel.' She missed Mabel. So I told her I saw Mabel now and then and talked to her all the time and I asked Hermione if she'd like to come up to the country if I arranged it, and she did. So I had Mabel and Hermione and some other people who were vaguely connected to show business, and Teak DaCosta [Morton DaCosta, director of musicals]. Later I asked Hermione, 'Did you enjoy the party?' She said, 'Oh, it was nice to see Mabel and Teak.' She didn't like it that I'd asked those other people."

Somehow Mabel managed to find the strength to travel to New York in November to tape a show for National Public Radio, one of a series called *Eileen Farrell's American Popular*

Singers, produced by the South Carolina Educational Radio Network. Loonis McGlohon not only co-hosted the show but also accompanied Mabel and Eileen Farrell with his trio. Mabel and McGlohon had become very close, and she had visited him and his wife in North Carolina on several occasions. Recalls McGlohon, "Usually after dinner, she'd say, 'Let's learn some new songs, or relearn some old songs.'"

"We were supposed to do a concert at the Dorothy Chandler Pavilion, although we later postponed it and it never took place. We were preparing for that. And one afternoon, rather late, she said, 'I want to relearn 'Once Upon a Summertime.' She had known the song, had done it, but it had slipped out of mind. It's a Michel LeGrand tune with a Johnny Mercer lyric, sort of a strange song. Mercer translated the lyric from the French and tried to stick very close to it. It goes, 'Once upon a summertime, I fell in love. . . ,' that kind of thing. It's about a young girl in love and she listens to the village church bells in her small town in France. Near the end of the song, the girl is trying to describe how it is being in love, once upon a summertime (I think it's a lost love, so she's really looking back to the past). The line goes: 'I felt as though the mayor had offered me the key to Paris.'

"Now, that's a strange line, and Mabel was having trouble with it. She'd say the line—say it rather than sing it. She'd say to me, 'Don't play.' I'd play up to that line, and she'd say, 'No, wait a minute, let me get this. I need to shape this line.' She'd say it. She'd move the emphasis from one word to the other, and she was not happy at all. She said, 'This is such a strange line.' And finally she said, 'Oh, I think I have it. It's very preposterous that the mayor of Paris would ever give a young girl in love a key to the city. It's just so unlikely that it has to strike this girl as being very funny.' Finally, she got it. Mabel had a little giggle that she sometimes put into the reading of a song. And then she made a gesture. She'd take the four fingers of one hand and put them up against her bottom lip, just under, a little pressure there. Seems so insignificant, but this woman spends all this time trying to shape this one line, and I kept thinking I wonder why Mercer used this line—it's really kind of a dumb line—until finally she did it, with that laugh that she could do. And suddenly, you knew what she was trying to say. She was trying to make this line make sense to somebody, because an eighteen-year-old girl would think that's pretty crazy, and come up with this image.

"Mabel was an actress. She said that every song was a one-act play. I learned something from her. She told me that she didn't think the melody was all that important in a song, it was the lyric. She said if the lyric was great, you could do a song. I'm afraid most singers hear the melody first, and the lyric second.

"Mabel always listened to the lyric. Another time she said, 'Something I've never done in my life, but have always loved, is the Kerry Dance.' I thought that was rather strange. I looked at her straight and said, 'Mabel, I can't imagine you doing the Kerry Dance.' She said, 'It's one of the saddest, most poignant songs ever written. It's about lost youth. No, I wouldn't want to do it as a jig. It's very slow.' So we did it very slow, and it was a very moving piece the way she did it."

"She loved contemporary music, too. One song she fell in love with in the last couple of years of her life was a Sergio Mendez song called 'So Many Stars.' "

She also kept up with contemporary musicians. Says McGlohon, "One of her favorite musicians in the whole world was a young Portuguese accordion player named Ed Montero —I suspect he was among her top five favorite musicians. I had never heard of him, and we were having dinner in New York and she said, 'After dinner, we must go and hear my favorite musician. You won't believe it.' I thought we were going to hear Oscar Peterson or somebody. She said, 'It's a young guy named Ed Montero. He plays accordion.' I said, 'Oh, Mabel, I don't want to hear an accordionist.' She said, 'You've never heard anything like this in your life.'

"We had an apartment in New York and had invited a few

friends over—Johnny Hartman and his wife, Teddy, and Marlene and Billy Verplanck, Teddi King and her husband Josh
Gerber—and we all went to Cleo's to hear this accordionist.
And at Cleo's, Sylvia Sims came in with Ruth Ellington [Duke
Ellington's sister], and there were so many of us that the manager, who of course knew Mabel, arranged sort of a horseshoe
of chairs around the stage. The performer was a girl from Brazil
or somebody—I wouldn't want to use her name—and she was
not very good. Everything she sang was sad and about death
and the end of love. We were waiting impatiently for Ed Montero to come out so we could hear him. We sat through this
girl's show and everybody was polite—nobody talked—but we
were all hoping she'd get the hell off. When it came to the end
of her act, we all applauded with a lot of bravado. She was
anxious to see who was doing all this applauding, so she walked
out of the spotlight, which was blinding her, and I think she
saw Sylvia Sims first and was startled. And then she saw Ruth
Ellington, and then her eyes moved from right to left and when
she got to Mabel, her eyes got large and she had to grab a chair
to support herself. Can you imagine coming off a show and
seeing the best singers in New York and in the center the lady
herself? She came over to Mabel and dropped to the floor, did a
curtsey, and kissed Mabel's hand. She said, 'Oh, Miss Mercer,
Miss Mercer, to think that you have come to hear me!' And
Mabel said, 'You were wonderful, darling.' Later that night, I
said, 'Mabel, that was such a generous thing for you to do.'
She said, 'Well, why not?' Not many people would have done
that. A lot of people would have said, 'We've been waiting for
you to get off.' But not Mabel. Mabel was kind to everybody."

The radio program with Eileen Farrell, which aired in January 1983, was so successful that in June, McGlohon produced
a program that again paired Mabel with Farrell at Alice Tully
Hall as part of the Kool Jazz Festival. Called "Listen to the
Words," it featured a number of songs on which Mabel recited
the verse, creating a situation and an ambience, and Eileen Farrell sang the choruses. Farrell also sang alone, and Mabel did

two recitations—"Christopher Robin's Prayer" and Edna St. Vincent Millay's "The Ballad of the Harp Weaver."

Recalls McGlohon, "I'm sure that there were those who thought it was very maudlin and cloying to do something like 'The Ballad of the Harp Weaver,' but the way Mabel did it, it was very emotional. Word had got out that she was in New York doing the show with Eileen Farrell, and the control room was full of all the singers in New York—Balder Lee, Marlene Verplanck, Johnny Hartman, Larry Carr, Buddy Barnes. When she finished that piece, there was absolute silence, and I looked through the glass and everyone was weeping openly. These were professionals, used to hearing performers."

Sunday Morning, the CBS show with Charles Kuralt, did a feature on the collaboration between Mabel Mercer and Eileen Farrell. "Mabel never saw it," says McGlohon. "She never would watch herself on television, always had an excuse. She said, 'You know, I meant to watch it, and then I fell asleep in the chair.' "

Among those who did watch Mabel on the *Sunday Morning* show was John Langley, the principal of the junior high school in Rockingham, North Carolina, about seven miles away from Charlotte, where McGlohon lives. "He puts on an arts festival for the children every year," says McGlohon. "He says he knows that without this experience the children would never see anything more cultural than a rock concert, that they will never in their lives see a ballet or hear a jazz group or anything like that. So for two weeks every year he brings in artists and craftspeople and performers—he has pewterers and wood-carvers and goldsmiths the first week and then the second week is all performing arts. He brings in big names. After that *Sunday Morning* show with Charles Kuralt he called me. He said, 'Loonis, how do I get in touch with Mabel Mercer?' I said, 'Well, Mabel lives in New York.' He said, 'Well, you wanna call her and ask if she can come down to do my arts festival?' I said, 'I don't think so.' I didn't want to put him down, but, first of all, this was an elderly lady and not terribly well, and then I didn't think

Mabel would be comfortable performing for junior high kids. He said, 'I never saw her before *Sunday Morning*, but I have never seen anybody communicate like that lady. Don't undersell my kids. They would dig her, and they would know what she's doing.' So, I said I'd ask her.

"We were in New York about two weeks after that, having dinner with Mabel, and I told her the story. I thought it was funny. I remember telling the man, 'Can you imagine Mabel Mercer in Rockingham, North Carolina?' I mean, here's a lady who's never performed anywhere in her life but London and Paris and New York and San Francisco. So, we told Mabel the story, thinking it would amuse her. She said, 'Do you think the children would loff'—she said loff—'at me?' I said, 'Mabel, nobody would ever laugh at you.' She said, 'Well then, I'd love to do it.' "

McGlohon helped her prepare. "She wanted to do a railroad song, of all things—'Run for the Roadhouse, Nellie.' She thought it would be a cute song. She hadn't done it for years but she had recorded it. She said, 'Why don't you get the drummer [in McGlohon's trio] to do the chookachooka kind of train sound.' So I found a recording that she'd done, and she had to listen to it. This was painful for her. She'd look up and say, 'Whoever told that old lady she could sing?' She also didn't like to talk about herself. She got very embarrassed. Her hands would flutter around her face. She didn't like to be told she was anything special.

"Anyway, Mabel went to Rockingham. You know, she always sat in a very elegant chair. They couldn't find any in Rockingham. So finally my wife, Nan, went to a furniture store and got kind of a brocade chair. Mabel sat in the chair. I introduced her. I didn't want to sell her too hard to these kids, because I'd worked with this audience many times before. They are exceptional. When John Langley tells them he's bringing in somebody good, they know it's somebody good, even though it may not be anything they'd like. He tells them, 'You may not like this, but I want you to listen and hang on to every note and every word, because years from now you may look back and say, 'That was a wonderful experience and thank God I got to hear that person.' So, her first number, yes, the audience was very tentative. There were about eight hundred kids, thirteen years old or so, and they had never heard of Mabel Mercer. I introduced her by saying, 'You know, this lady is from England, and she has something about her that's unusual enough so that one of the very staid and formal London newspapers said when she went back recently to play there, after being away for many years, they said, "For the first time in British history two queens are in residence at the same time—Elizabeth at Buckingham and Mabel Mercer at the Savoy." We opened the curtains and Mabel did her first number, and as I said, the audience was somewhat tentative. Mabel was very nervous during the last half of that first song, whatever it was, I don't even remember, and we all felt the tension.

"I had said to her, 'I think for the second number you ought to do something that the kids might have heard,' so she did 'Both Sides Now,' and during that second number it was very obvious that the kids knew something very special was happening on that stage, and by the end of it Mabel had won that audience over. They gave her two standing ovations during the performance, and I remember looking out from the front and seeing the superintendent of the North Carolina schools, who had come over from Raleigh, and some other adults, and the tears were streaming down their faces.

"Driving back from this little show in Rockingham, Mabel was very quiet. Then she said, 'You know, I think I received my favorite compliment today.' We said, 'What was that?' She said, 'Well, as I was leaving, a little black boy, a very tiny boy, came up and touched my hand and looked up at me and said, "Miss Mercer, you done *good*." ' "

That same year, 1983, President Ronald Reagan expressed similar sentiments when he presented Mabel with the Presidential Medal of Freedom at the White House. Adde Wallin-Beach recalls, "When she called me and asked if I would go with her, I was excited, but she wasn't. She said, 'I don't understand it. Why am I selected? There are so many more worthy people.' I said, 'Because you have done so much for the music world, Mabel.'

"I helped her fix the dress she wore to the White House. It was one she had made—she made all her dresses and all her shawls, and Ena Boucher used to help her make them, but by this time Ena was ill and didn't come up very often—and Mabel had lost weight, so it had to be taken in. It was all gored, and you couldn't just take one in, you had to take a little tiny bit of each one, all across.

"By the time we got to Washington, she was excited. Muriel Finch and I went with her, and my nephew was in the Secret Service at the White House then, and he came over to the hotel and took us to the White House and he took Muriel and me to some of the rooms that we otherwise could not have gone to.

"In addition to Mabel, there were other recipients—Billy Graham and Jacob Javits and George Balanchine and Bear Bryant. They had a big round table with the President and the recipients, and then other round tables. The recipients were introduced, and then they went up separately and he presented each one with the medal and then they all stood in line."

Mabel's citation read: "Mabel Mercer has been called a living testament to the artfulness of the American song, and a legend if there ever was one. Her talent, her elegance and her unique way with a lyric have gathered a devoted following all over the world. Her special style has influenced some of America's most famous performers, earning her the reputation of a singer's singer. Miss Mercer's career has spanned more than sixty years and she continues to delight audiences and critics alike. With her incomparable talent she has helped shape and enrich American music."

Continues Adde Wallin-Beach, "On the train going back, I said to her, 'Don't you feel a little like flying?' She said, 'I sort of don't believe this all happened.' Then we got to New York and they had a big party that night for her at the Algonquin—

Don Smith arranged it. Mabel often stayed there gratis. We used to stay there occasionally at half-rate, which was still steep for my pocketbook. When we got up to her room, she said, 'This is just too much for me. I'm just so exhausted.' Months later, someone said to her, 'You received the highest award an American citizen can receive from the President.' She said, 'I did?' You'd tell her, but it didn't dawn on her. She wasn't a person that expected any of this."

Harry Beard did not accompany Mabel to Washington, although Mabel would like to have shared the honor with him. By this time, his health was far too poor. Says Will Craik, "He was on L-dopa, and this had very unpleasant side effects at times, but he would usually stay in his room if he didn't feel well, and when he felt better he would come out. He didn't go to New York anymore. He was very proud of his appearance—he used to go to New York just to get a haircut—and he didn't want people to see him shaking and thin. He couldn't handle things anymore, only by phone. It was very difficult for him to write. Mabel was very protective of him, would help him in and out of cars and all."

Remembers Adde Wallin-Beach, "She called one day and said, 'I can't wake Harry up. Will you come right down?' What he had done was, he had gotten up, gone to the bathroom, started to dress and maybe didn't feel good and came back and fell back on his bed, because he had his underwear and shirt on."

While Mabel had known how ill Harry was, it was still difficult for her to adjust to his being gone. "She was just devastated," says Adde Wallin-Beach. "His sister Pearl came for the funeral, but Mabel did not want her to go through his things at that time. She said, 'Just leave everything of Harry's as it is,' and so Pearl went back to California without going through any of it. In fact, Pearl did not go through Harry's things until after Mabel died. Then, she stayed with me for about two months while we went through boxes and boxes of Harry's. There were a lot of little notes and cards and letters, and there was one card that, I think, he had intended to give to Mabel, for her birthday or something, but never had. It said, 'Your song is in my heart. Love, Harry.' "

Harry lived on in Mabel's heart, and his name was often on her lips. Says Adde Wallin-Beach, "She was always saying, 'Harry took care of this,' or, 'Harry said this,' or, 'If Harry could see me now.' We'd decide to go into town and she'd be dressed for working in the yard, and she'd look down and say, 'Oh, Harry'd just flip if he saw the way I'm going into town.' Harry used to tell her how to dress; we would be going out to dinner, or she would have an engagement, and she'd come downstairs and he would say, 'I don't like that one on you; put on the pink, or the green.' Mabel and I were sitting in the kitchen one day and a little field mouse came in, and she said, 'Oh, good thing Harry is no longer with us.' "

Mabel decided that the best way to cope with the loss of Harry was to go back to work. In fact, by the time she was honored at the White House, Mabel was preparing a retrospective called "An Evening With Mabel Mercer," in which she would review in story and song the highlights of her career. It was her own version of her autobiography, a print version of which she did not care to write. Naturally, she was approached by several people about such a memoir, but she always declined. Says Will Craik, "Mabel often said, 'Not while I'm alive. My private life is my private life. But once I'm gone, they can write anything they want about me. Let's just hope they'll be kind.' I heard her tell three or four people, 'Not when I'm alive, dear. You can wait until I'm gone and then you can write anything you like.' " Mabel was also superstitious about such things—Adde Wallin-Beach recalls that in the late 1970s or early 1980s Mabel stated that she did not want to make a will because she would surely die as soon as the document was drawn up—and it is likely that she had similar fears about an autobiography.

Loonis McGlohon helped her prepare her musical story. The two were often together in Mabel's last years. Sometimes she would visit him and his wife in Charlotte. "She loved to come in the spring of the year. She thought Charlotte was beautiful. She was so unlike the lady we saw onstage—that glamorous lady in the throne chair. She loved to put on blue jeans and garden. On the last visit here—she was here for about two weeks—every afternoon she'd say, 'We must go take a drive, I want to see the flowers again.' She was like a child looking at all the azaleas. She once said, 'My God, do you know that you live in a beautiful green park?'

"In the last few years of her life she began to do poems and poetry readings. She felt her voice was strong and that this was something she could do. She was very religious, as you know, and she wanted very much to record the New Testament. She said, 'I'd just like you to play the piano very quietly behind me.' So I talked to Sinatra about it one night, and he thought it was a wonderful idea. Obviously, it had to be produced and would be an expensive project and would take a long time, because Mabel wanted to record the *whole* New Testament. I wanted to get it done very badly, but we just never got it going, and I was very disappointed that the thing she wanted to do most of all in the last few years of her life she was never able to do."

Father Lee Smith would also have liked to hear Mabel recording something biblical. "I remember when my sister died and we were having a memorial Mass and I invited Mabel and she came. I asked if she would do a reading and she said, 'Oh, my dear, I don't have my glasses.' But she borrowed Willie's and she read the Song of Solomon. I had never heard the English language spoken like that, and we hoped to record Mabel reading Psalms. She had a great following among priests. They are not married, they are celibate, but they are passionate men, and Mabel touched them. She touched them because she understood what life was all about, she was celebrating life, and you can't do that unless you are a spiritual person."

Mabel's last performances were benefits for the SLE Foundation, which combats lupus erythematosus—the nightclub singer Teddi King, a good friend of Mabel's, had died of that disease, and Mabel was pleased to do benefits for the foundation. Before these performances, Mabel and McGlohon would rehearse in New York. "The last thing we did was a lupus benefit at the Grand Hyatt Hotel," says McGlohon. "It was in November, about five months before she died, and it was her last performance, and strangely enough it was one of her best performances in the later years. On the NPR show back in '77–'78, she was doing more parlando than singing, but she was really singing at the last four she did for the lupus benefit—she sounded like she did twenty years ago. It was rather amazing, because I remember she was tired at rehearsal that afternoon—we rehearsed up at Mitch Miller's apartment on Central Park West —and she was a little irritable. This happened all the time in her later years. When she was tired, she would not do well in rehearsal. Then suddenly, when she got onstage there was this energy that came. I think that's true with a lot of performers, but it was rather strange to watch because I would have never bet at rehearsal that she could pull off a great performance. That night at the performance some kind of magic happened. When she got onstage she looked absolutely radiant, and she sang as well as I'd heard her sing in years and years.

"She did the Kerry Dance, I remember. And the last song she sang was one she had introduced—'While We're Young' by Alec Wilder. He wrote it around 1941. It's really sad—'Songs were made to sing while we're young/Every day is spring while we're young. . . . /Time flies so fast . . . /So blue the skies, all sweet surprise/shines before our eyes while/we're young.' It's saying, 'Hold on to it.' It probably wouldn't have been a standard at all if not for Mabel. It was the last song she ever performed.

"I remember William Livingstone, editor of *Stereo Review*, was sitting at the table, and when she came down, he said, 'Mabel, you sound just the way you did years ago.' She had discarded the parlando and was really singing, singing all the notes. I think it was some kind of inner strength that came through. Her performances were always good, never mediocre, but this was a fantastic performance, and I'm grateful that the last one she did she could not have been embarrassed by. It was wonderful."

By January, Mabel was in the hospital. "The angina," says Will Craik. "Usually it's a periodic thing—you take a nitroglycerin tablet and it goes away. But hers was uninterrupted and they had all kinds of tubes in her. Muriel Finch would take me over—we'd go every day. And one day we were sitting there in the hospital and Muriel asked, 'What do you want to take with you when we go to the West Coast?' I nearly went into cardiac arrest. It seemed Mabel had this thing scheduled out on the West Coast with Eileen Farrell and Muriel was going to take her there. Muriel said, 'The doctor said it would be all right, if she felt up to it.' But all you had to do was look at Mabel to know she wasn't up to it. I had a vision of Muriel getting her out in California somewhere and that would be the end of Mabel.

"Mabel felt very guilty because she was letting these people in California down. I said, 'Well, make up your mind, dear. Would you rather disappoint somebody or kill yourself? Which?' So, she didn't go. Later, I told Muriel, 'Listen, I've been through this, up to and including the open heart surgery.' Muriel said, 'Well, she's never happy unless she's working.' It was true. Mabel liked to work if she had things she wanted to do—to the house. And she was always afraid there wouldn't be enough for dinner tomorrow. I trace this back to her childhood—I don't know if they were in dire poverty, but there wasn't an abundance of things, let's put it that way. And Mabel never felt secure.

"Almost to the end she had that 'emergency ration' in the cupboard, in the corner of the kitchen. It had been there as long as I had known her, and one day I happened to go by it and there was an awful smell. I made a mistake, I opened it. Pandora's box it wasn't. The mice had been nesting in there for twenty years—she had cans of dog and cat food in there, and cans of beef stew (in case she couldn't get out to shop in winter).

There was mouse dung all over and it stank. I took it outside to clean it out, and I'd pick up a can and it would just crumble in my hand. When she came up and saw that I had emptied it, she was furious—'Where is my emergency ration?' I told her, 'It isn't, dear, unless you're going to eat rust.' There was nothing—cans of sauerkraut had just disintegrated when you touched them.''

Craik understood Mabel's desire both to continue working and to meet her commitments. "But going to California in her condition was ridiculous."

Naturally, Mabel worried over the hospital bills. "She had insurance—Blue Cross and Medicare," says Craik. "She had worked again and had money in the bank. Joe Carstairs was very helpful. Mabel came out of the hospital, and I went over and stayed with her for about a week toward the end of January. Meanwhile, this was all kept very hush-hush because some of her friends up there felt that Mabel wouldn't want people to know she was sick. But Mabel was beginning to wonder why she wasn't getting any cards, or telephone calls. I finally said, 'This nonsense about keeping it hush-hush is going to end. I'm telling everybody I know.' ''

On January 31, 1984, Bricktop died, in her sleep, in her apartment in New York. Mabel was told, and asked her friend Father Lee Smith to call and express her condolences. She was unable to attend the funeral.

Because of Mabel's age, the doctors would not operate on her, and although her angina attacks continued there was little they could do but treat her and release her. "It was amazing," says Will Craik. "She would have these spells and then she would bounce right back and the next day you'd go in and she'd be chatting and laughing and watching TV. I remember one day she was quite pleased. I was there with her and this young orderly came in with something to put on her table—fresh water or something—and he said, 'You're Miss Mercer, aren't you?' And she said, 'Yes,' and he said, 'You don't remember me, do you? I helped build your garage.' This neighbor, Mr. Macready, had been a manual training teacher and in the summer he would take three or four boys into his home and take them on various construction projects. They built Mabel's garage, and this youngster had been one of them. She was so pleased. She said, 'How did you remember me?' She couldn't understand how anybody would remember *her*.

In February and March, Mabel was feeling better, and during this time she attended a dinner party given for her by her neighbor Judy Juhring. Ronny Whyte was there. "After dinner we went into the parlor and were kidding around, as we always did. I sat down at the piano and said, 'Mabel, will you do so and so?' and I started to sing and she started singing along. She sang three or four songs, and it was the last time she ever sang because a week later she was in the hospital and two weeks or so after that she was gone."

Will Craik recalls, "I don't know if Mabel realized how ill she was or not, but right up to the end she was not going to make a will. . . . But she was in the hospital, in early April I think, and we were there, and she went into cardiac arrest. She was lying in bed and the pain was so intense that it just threw her up, so she was sitting upright. The call went out—Mayday, Mayday—and they got her stabilized. But I told Muriel, 'We gotta get a lawyer in here.'

"We got Dick Alford. Pearl had hired him to take care of Harry's affairs, so Mabel sort of knew him. Finally, on a Thursday, I talked to Mabel. I said, 'Listen, dear, you've got to do something. Otherwise, Uncle Mario [Governor Cuomo] is going to get the whole thing. The animals will get nothing; he'll be able to take the property and level it and make a parking lot out of it if he wants to. The doctor says it can go either way' —I tried to break it to her gently—'and please, for our peace of mind, tell us how you want it in case anything serious happens.' Of course the poor dear hated to do it, but she agreed, and we drew up the will, though it was a week or so before she signed it.

"People visited her. Dicky [Graden] was too ill to travel

then, but Ena [Boucher] came up, a member of her church drove her up. Adde was in Mexico and I didn't realize no one had told her. [Adde Wallin-Beach did manage to get back to Mabel before she died.] Other people came. Finally, Mabel signed her will. She would seize any opportunity to postpone it—it was bad luck to make a will. She would die immediately. But of course she put it off so long that she did. . . . It was not because of the superstition, it was because she just procrastinated so long."

Father Lee Smith "anointed her in the hospital. And while she was there I called the White House and said she'd been a recipient of the Medal of Freedom and was in the hospital in Pittsfield; I asked for a get-well card to be sent. She was thrilled that Ronald and Nancy Reagan had sent her a get-well card. But the big thrill at the hospital was that Frank Sinatra had called. They brought a phone in for Mabel to speak to Frank."

Mabel died the day after she signed her will. "The next day, they called us in the morning and said she had passed away," says Will Craik. "They didn't explain the circumstances to us. It was six-thirty or seven o'clock."

Mabel was gone. It was hard for her friends to believe. Rosetta LeNoire remembers, "When she died, I was in the hospital, and they had kept a lot of things from me. I found out that Mabel had died when the calls started coming in on my private phone—from Florida and Georgia—and do you know that these people were crying on the phone? They kept thanking me and blessing me. One woman said, 'You know, if I die and get to heaven and you're not there, I'm gonna picket, because you took me to see Mabel. I can't tell you how great I felt.' And they weren't lying."

On Friday, April 24, 1984, the largest funeral ever held in the small upcountry community paid tribute to Mabel. After calling hours at the Wenk Funeral Home, Mabel's casket was taken to St. James Church and carried up the aisle by the active pallbearers, including Adde Wallin-Beach's son, Peter. Among the honorary pallbearers, the biggest names—Tony Bennett,

Sammy Davis, Jr., Johnny Mathis, Rex Reed, and Bobby Short—were not there. But Bart Howard, Jimmy Lyon, Loonis McGlohon, and Will Craik were, as were Ronny Whyte, Anne Francine, J. Billy and Marlene Verplanck, the Reverend Peter O'Brien, Adde Wallin-Beach, Muriel Finch, Donald Smith, Ena Boucher, and Dicky Graden, and more than two hundred others.

Several of Mabel's priest friends eulogized her, among them the Reverend Joseph Sinisky, pastor of St. James Church, the Reverend Lee Smith of New York City and Chatham Centre, and the Reverends James Hinckey and Dennis Corrado of the Cathedral of St. James in Brooklyn. Father Corrado ended his eulogy by playing Mabel's recording of Alec Wilder's "While We're Young," and tears flowed freely in the little church.

Then a mile-long cortege of cars made its way from the church to the steeply inclined Red Rock cemetery, where the grass was beginning to show signs of green and the somnolent lilac bushes were in bud, and as rain fell softly on her friends Mabel was laid to rest next to Harry Beard in the earth that she had so profoundly loved.

Mabel's mother had died many years earlier and left her property in Williamstown, New York, to Mabel. Mabel, in turn, bequeathed that property to the Millennium Guild, in care of Pegeen Fitzgerald, the veteran New York radio personality, "to be used or sold and the proceeds used for the care of animals." Says Will Craik, "Mabel had a little painting, by the bar in the den, of her mother's 'house,' as she called it. It was really a little cottage, by a pond. Her mother had painted it. Mabel left the acreage up there to Pegeen Fitzgerald's animal league. She always had the idea that they were going to turn all the stray dogs and cats loose up there, and let them just run and play. Adde took her up there once, and Adde said, 'You know, it was not a very valuable piece of property.' It was quite run down. They probably should have sold it and used the money."

The remainder of Mabel's estate was divided equally among Madeleine "Dicky" Graden and Ena Boucher, her "adopted sisters" (Ena Boucher died shortly after Mabel did), the United Negro College Fund ("to be used for scholarships to be given in my name in the field of music"), and to the Morris Memorial facility ("to the children of the Chatham, New York, area"). According to a spokesman for the Morris Memorial, the income would approximate four thousand dollars annually.

Mabel did not leave a large estate, but what she did have she left primarily to young people and animals, those of God's creatures who are the most vulnerable. She made no provision for her personal effects. There was an auction of her belongings. Some of her papers were given to the Schomburg Center for Research in Black Culture in New York City. Some of her friends grumble that her estate was not handled properly.

On a Sunday in June 1984, Mabel's friends and admirers gathered at Town Hall to pay tribute to her memory. There were a number of spoken and musical tributes. "The whole saloon brigade is here tonight," announced actress Dorothy Loudon, and indeed, for one evening the magic of the era over which Mabel had reigned was revived. Bobby Short and Cy Coleman did a couple of lighthearted piano and vocal duets. Sylvia Sims remembered being taken to see Mabel by Billie Holiday, who told her, "You have got to hear this fancy singer." Carol Hall, whose song "Jenny Rebecca" Mabel recorded, remembered discovering that Mabel was listed in the *Manhattan Telephone Directory* and that when she had called to ask if Mabel would like to hear her songs, Mabel had said yes. Jimmy Lyon did a piano medley of "Wait Till You See Her" and "The Most Beautiful Girl in the World." Buddy Barnes played an energetic rendition of "All by Myself." Marlene Verplanck, accompanied by Loonis McGlohon, sang McGlohon's "Songbird," and Bart Howard performed "It Was Worth It," the song he had written for Mabel nearly thirty-five years before. Toward the end of the evening, a recording of Mabel singing "Time Heals Everything" in a voice close to tears summed up the feelings of most of those who were there.

They included Rosetta LeNoire and Julius Monk. "Joe Carstairs was there that evening," says Monk. "I saw her in the distance with Bart Howard and I was absolutely electrified when I saw her. I hadn't seen her since her farewell at the Hotel Pierre. I'm very reluctant to contact people at this stage of the game because our lives have gone in such separate directions. I'm one of the last of that breed. Jimmy Daniels is dead. Jacoby's gone. Garland Wilson is dead—he died in the Boeuf sur le Toit in Paris, where he had returned after being at the Bon Soir for so many years, as well as the Ruban Bleu. Doris Duke I know made a welcome contribution to get Garland's remains back here."

In February 1985, Donald Smith organized yet another tribute to Mabel, this time in celebration of her eighty-fifth birthday. It was held on the St. Regis Roof, where her seventy-fifth birthday had been celebrated. Titled "Once in a Blue Moon—Mabel Mercer: A Cabaret Celebration," it benefited the newly established Mabel Mercer Foundation to help young performers who wished to pursue the special field to which Mabel had devoted her life.

But there will never be another Mabel Mercer.

A

A Partial List
of
Songs Sung
by
Mabel Mercer

Ace In The Hole (Porter) 1941
After You (Porter) 1932
All In Fun (Kern–Hammerstein) 1939
All Of You (Porter) 1954
Autumn Leaves (Mercer–Prevert–Kosma) 1950
Bad Is For Other People (Coleman–Wells) 1966
The Ballad Of The Sad Young Men (Landesmann–Wolf) 1959
Be A Child (Wilder)
Being Green (Raposo) 1970
Big Fat Heart (Coleman–Fields) 1971
Blame It On My Youth (Levant–Heyman) 1933
Both Sides Now (Mitchell) 1967
By Myself (Dietz–Schwartz) 1937

Carry Me Back To Old Manhattan (Cory-Cross)
Charm (Roy) 1953
Chase Me Charlie (Coward) 1950
Children In The Carousel (Gavin-Gavin)
Come Rain Or Come Shine (Mercer-Arlen) 1946
Confession (Dietz-Schwartz) 1931
Dancing On The Ceiling (Rodgers-Hart) 1931
Did You Ever Cross Over To Sneden's (Wilder) 1947
The Door Opened (Howard) 1940
Early Morning Blues (Coleman-McCarthy) 1960
Echoes Of My Life (Wilder)
End Of A Love Affair (Redding) 1950
Everybody Has The Right To Be Wrong (Coleman)
Ev'ry Time We Say Goodbye (Porter) 1944
Experiment (Porter) 1933
Falling In Love With Love (Rodgers-Hart) 1938
The Fifth Of July (Roy)
The Fifty-Ninth Street Bridge Song (Simon) 1966
The First Warm Day In May (Howard) 1951
Fly Me To The Moon (Howard) 1954
The Folks Who Live On The Hill (Hammerstein-Kern) 1937
Goodbye, John (Wilder) 1950
Grow Tall, My Son (McGlohon) 1963
Guess I'll Go Back Home This Summer (Robison) 1939
Hello, My Lover, Goodbye (Green-Heyman) 1931
Hello, Young Lovers (Rodgers-Hammerstein) 1951
Here I Sit In My Rocking Chair
Here's To Us (Coleman-Leigh) 1962
He Was Too Good To Me (Rodgers-Hart) 1930
How Deep Is The Ocean (Berlin) 1932
How Do You Say Auf Wiedersehen (Mercer)
How Little We Know (Carmichael-Mercer) 1956
I'm All Smiles (Leonard-Martin) 1964
I Am Ashamed That Women Are So Simple (Porter) 1948
I'm Glad I'm Not Young Anymore (Lerner-Loewe) 1958
I'm Watching You (Coleman) 1959
I Can't Give You Anything But Love (McHugh-Fields) 1928
I Loves You Porgy (Gershwin) 1959
I've Got Your Number (Coleman-Leigh) 1962

If Love Were All (Coward) 1929
If You Leave Paris (Howard) 1938
I See It Now (Wilder)
Is It Always Like This (Wilder) 1943
Isn't He Adorable (Coleman-McCarthy) 1960
Isn't It A Pity (Gershwin) 1933
It All Depends On You (DeSylva-Brown-Henderson) 1925
It Amazes Me (Coleman) 1958
It Happens All Over The World (Cory-Cross)
It's A Lie, It's A Fake! (Fogarty-Engvick) 1953
It's All Right With Me (Porter) 1953
It's Delovely (Porter) 1936
It's So Peaceful In The Country (Wilder) 1941
It Was Worth It (Howard) 1950
Ivory Tower (Cory-Cross) 1956
I Walk A Little Faster (Coleman) 1957
I'll Be Around (Wilder) 1942
I'll Be Seeing You (Kahal-Fain) 1938
Jenny Rebecca (Hall) 1965
Just In Time (Styne-Comden-Green) 1956
Just Once Around The Clock (Romberg-Hammerstein) 1935
Just One Of Those Things (Porter) 1935
The Kerry Dance (Irish folk song)
The Last Time I Saw Paris (Kern-Hammerstein) 1940
Lazy Afternoon (LaTouche-Moross) 1954
Let Me Love You (Howard) 1954
Let Me Show You My New York (Whyte) 1967
Let's Begin (Kern-Harbach) 1933
Little Girl Blue (Rodgers-Hart) 1935
Little Grey Home In The West (Eardley-Wilmot-Lohr) 1911
Lonely Little Boy (Clements)
Looking At You (Porter) 1929
Love For Sale (Porter) 1930
Love Wise (Fischer-Elmslie)
Lucky To Be Me (Bernstein-Comden-Green) 1944
Mandy (Berlin) 1919
Matelot (Coward) 1945
Mira (Merrill) 1961
More I Cannot Wish You (Loesser) 1950

The Most Beautiful Girl In The World (Rodgers-Hart) 1935
My Funny Valentine (Rodgers-Hart) 1937
My Heart Stood Still (Rodgers-Hart) 1927
My Love Is A Wanderer (Howard) 1952
My Melancholy Baby (Norton-Burnett) 1912
My Resistance Is Low (Carmichael) 1951
My Romance (Rodgers-Hart) 1935
Nobody Else But Me (Hammerstein-Kern) 1946
The Olive Tree (Wilder)
Once In A Blue Moon (Kern-Caldwell) 1923
Once Upon A Summertime (LeGrand-Mercer) 1962
Once Upon A Time (Adams-Strouse) 1962
One For The Money (Steininger-Brown) 1947
Ours (Porter) 1936
Over The Weekend (Brooks-McCarthy) 1932
Poor Pierrot (Kern-Harbach) 1931
Remind Me (Kern-Fields) 1940
The Riviera (Coleman-McCarthy) 1957
Round House Nellie (Robison)
Run To Love (Fisher-Segal)
Sail Away (Coward) 1961
Season's Greetings (Warren)
Sell Me (Howard) 1957
Send In The Clowns (Sondheim) 1973
September Song (Anderson-Weill) 1938
So In Love (Porter) 1948
So Many Stars (Mendez)
Some Fine Day (Walter)
Some Other Time (Bernstein-Comden-Green) 1944
Songbird (McGlohon) 1978
Sonnet (Cory-Cross)
Staying Young (Merrill) 1959
Summertime (Heyward-Gershwin) 1935
Sunday In New York (Nelson) 1959
Sunday In Savannah (MacKay)
Sweet Talk (Coleman-Huddleston) 1964
S'Wonderful (Gershwin) 1927
Symphony (Lawrence-Alstone) 1945
Thank You For The Flowers (Johnson-Moore) 1932
They All Fall In Love (Porter) 1929

This Is All I Ask (Jenkins) 1958
This Is Romance (Duke-Heyman)
Time Heals Everything (Herman)
To Be In Love! (Howard) 1957
Too Old To Die Young (Grand)
Trouble Comes (Fisher-Segal)
Trouble Is A Man (Wilder) 1944
Trouble Man (Weill-Anderson) 1949
Tu reviendras (Menotti) 1950
The Twelve Days of Christmas (Middle Ages carol)
Up The Hill In Red Rock (Wilder)
Use Your Imagination (Porter) 1950
Wait Till We're 65 (Lerner-Lane) 1965
Wait Till You See Her (Rodgers-Hart) 1942
Walk Up (Howard) 1956
The Way We Were (Bergman-Bergman-Hamlisch) 1973
What Is There To Say (Duke-Harburg) 1933
When In Rome, Do As The Romans Do (Coleman-Leigh) 1964
When Love Comes Your Way (Porter) 1935
When The World Was Young (Mercer) 1951
Where Oh Where (Porter) 1950
While We're Young (Wilder-Engvick-Palitz) 1943
Why Did I Choose You (Martin-Leonard) 1965
Who Wants To Fall In Love (Howard) 1953
Would You Believe It (Howard) 1952
Year After Year (Howard) 1955
You Are In Love (Hauerbach-Clark-Friml) 1916
You're Nearer (Rodgers-Hart) 1943
You Are Not My First Love (Howard) 1953
You Are Too Beautiful (Rodgers-Hart) 1958
You Better Go Now (Graham-Reichner) 1936
You Fascinate Me So (Coleman-Leigh) 1958
Young And Foolish (Horwitt-Hague) 1954
You Should See Yourself (Coleman-Fields) 1965
You Will Wear Velvet (Cory-Cross) 1954

Arnold Caplin, Judy Bell, Gene Grissom, Bart Howard, David Litofsky, The Welk Music Group/T. B. Harms Company, and Notable Music, Inc., provided materials for this list. ASCAP Index Service, The Library of the Theater and Music Collection, Museum of the City of New York, and The Lincoln Center Performing Arts Library were also helpful. Dates are given primarily for published songs.

APPENDIX

B

DISCOGRAPHY

Mabel Mercer Sings Decca DL4472
Songs By Mabel Mercer, Vol. 1 Atlantic ALS–402
Songs By Mabel Mercer, Vol. 2 Atlantic ALS–403
Songs By Mabel Mercer, Vol. 3 Songs Written for Mabel Mercer
    Atlantic ALS–408
Mabel Mercer Sings Cole Porter Atlantic ATL1213
Midnight At Mabel Mercer's Atlantic AT1244
Art of Mabel Mercer Atlantic 2–At.2–602
Once In a Blue Moon Atlantic ATL1301
Merely Marvelous Atlantic ATL1322
Mabel Mercer and Bobby Short at Town Hall Atlantic SD–2–604
Mabel Mercer For Always Stanyan (reissue of *Mabel Mercer* Sings)

A Tribute To Mabel Mercer on the Occasion of Her 75th Birthday
  Atlantic MM4-100 (four records; reissues of *Mabel Mercer Sings
  Cole Porter, Midnight at Mabel Mercer's, Once In a Blue Moon,*
  and *Merely Marvelous*
Echoes of My Life Audiophile AP161-162 (2 records)
*Mabel Mercer and Bobby Short at Town Hall, II: The Realm of Mercer
  and Short* Atlantic SD2-605

Notes and Sources

Chapter I. Mabel's First Years

1. S. Theodore Felstead, *Stars Who Made the Halls: A Hundred Years of English Humour, Harmony and Hilarity* (London: T. Werner Laurie Ltd., 1946), p. 32.
2. Ibid., pp. 42–43.
3. Ibid., p. 102.
4. Marian Zalian, "An Ageless Enchantress and Her Timeless Songs," *San Francisco Examiner & Chronicle*, January 29, 1978, p. 17.
5. Whitney Balliett, "Our Footloose Correspondents: In the Country," *The New Yorker*, September 6, 1982, p. 49.

6. Whitney Balliett, "Profiles: A Queenly Aura," *The New Yorker*, November 18, 1972, p. 60.
7. Ibid., p. 61.
8. Balliett, 1982, p. 49.
9. Zalian, p. 17.
10. William Livingstone, "Mabel Mercer: William Livingstone Visits With the Singer's Singer," *Stereo Review*, February 1975, p. 60.
11. Ibid.; also John S. Wilson, "Mabel Mercer, Phraser of Songs, Dies," *The New York Times*, April 21, 1984, p. 24.
12. Balliett, 1972, p. 58.
13. Balliett, 1982, p. 44.
14. Roland Wild, "She Never Looked Back," *Park East*, March 1953, p. 16.
15. Ibid., p. 17.
16. Felstead, p. 122.
17. Finis Farr, *Black Champion: The Life and Times of Jack Johnson* (New York: Charles Scribner's Sons, 1964), p. 62.
18. Livingstone, p. 62.
19. Wild, p. 19.
20. Livingstone, p. 62.
21. Ibid.
22. Felstead, p. 69.
23. Ibid., p. 100.
24. Ibid., p. 101.
25. Balliett, 1982, p. 44.
26. Wild, p. 19.
27. Livingstone, p. 62.
28. Robert Kimball and William Bolcom, *Reminiscing With Sissle and Blake* (New York: The Viking Press, 1973), p. 69.
29. Chris Goddard, *Jazz Away From Home* (New York: Paddington Press, 1979), pp. 19–20.
30. Balliett, 1982, p. 44.
31. Goddard, p. 298.
32. Balliett, 1972, p. 61.
33. Wild, p. 19.
34. Balliett, 1972, p. 61.
35. Livingstone, p. 62.
36. Wild, p. 19.

Chapter II. Paris, and Bricktop's

1. Harold P. Clunn, *The Face of Paris* (London: Spring Books, n.d.), p. 168.
2. Chris Goddard, *Jazz Away From Home* (New York: Paddington Press, 1979), p. 302.
3. "Mabel Mercer Sings,' *WPAT Gaslight Revue*, August 1964, p. 51. Adelaide Wallin-Beach collection.
4. Ibid.
5. Bricktop interview with Jim Haskins, December 16, 1981.
6. Ibid.
7. Roland Wild, "She Never Looked Back," *Park East*, March 1953, p. 19.
8. Danton Walker, "Broadway: Queen of Clubs," *New York Sunday News*, February 19, 1956, p. 10.
9. Bricktop interview.
10. Ibid., p. 101.
11. Ibid., p. 158.
12. Ibid., p. 159.
13. Ibid., p. 160.
14. Bricktop, p. 161.
15. Bricktop, with Jim Haskins, *Bricktop* (New York: Atheneum, 1983, p. 161.
16. Ibid., pp. 160–61.
17. *WPAT*, p. 51.
18. Whitney Balliett, "Profiles: A Queenly Aura," *The New Yorker*, November 18, 1972, p. 61.
19. *WPAT*, p. 51.
20. Wild, p. 20.
21. Robert Kimball, ed., *Cole* (New York: Holt, Rinehart & Winston, 1971), p. 104.
22. Copyright 1930, Harms, Inc.
23. William Livingstone, "Mabel Mercer: William Livingstone Visits With the Singer's Singer," *Stereo Review*, February 1975, p. 65.
24. Bricktop, p. 177.
25. Livingstone, p. 63.
26. Whitney Balliett, "Our Footloose Correspondents: In the Country," *The New Yorker*, September 6, 1982, p. 51.

27. Livingstone, p. 63.
28. Bricktop, pp. 173–74.
29. Livingstone, p. 63.
30. Bricktop, p. 219.
31. *WPAT*, p. 51.
32. Livingstone, p. 63.
33. Bricktop, p. 175.
34. Ibid., pp. 188–89.
35. Ibid., p. 192.
36. Balliett, 1982, p. 44.
37. Bricktop, p. 198.
38. Bricktop papers, Schomburg Center for Research in Black Culture.
39. Goddard, p. 244.
40. Bricktop papers.
41. Bricktop papers.

Chapter III. Wandering Chanteuse

1. William Livingstone, "Mabel Mercer: William Livingstone Visits With the Singer's Singer," *Stereo Review*, February 1975, pp. 65–66.
2. Lucius Beebe, "Cafe Society," *Hearst's International–Cosmopolitan*, April 1937, p. 38.
3. Ibid., May 1937, p. 84.
4. Livingstone, p. 63.
5. Bricktop, with Jim Haskins, *Bricktop* (New York: Atheneum Publishers, 1983), pp. 209–10.
6. Ibid., p. 214.
7. N.s., n.d. Mabel Mercer papers, Schomburg Center for Research in Black Culture.
8. Roland Wild, "She Never Looked Back," *Park East*, March 1953, p. 20.
9. Ibid.
10. Ibid.
11. Bricktop, p. 214.
12. Ibid.
13. Malcolm Johnson, "Cafe Life in New York," *The New York Sun*, July 1, 1942, n.p. Bricktop papers, Schomburg Center for Research in Black Culture.
14. "Cy Walter Dies; Cocktail Pianist," *The New York Times*,

August 20, 1968, n.p. Walter, vertical file, Lincoln Center
Library for the Performing Arts.

15. Ibid.
16. Bricktop, p. 214.
17. Ibid., p. 222.

Chapter IV. Tony's

1. Robert Sylvester, *No Cover Charge: A Backward Look at the
   Night Clubs* (New York: The Dial Press, 1956), pp. 83–84.
2. Jane Cobb, "The 1001 Night Clubs," *The New York Times*,
   January 12, 1941, p. 13.
3. Letter to Jim Haskins from John A. Morton, Jr., March 31,
   1986.
4. William Hawkins, " 'The Consul' Hits Where We Live," *New
   York World Telegram*, n.d., n.p. Mabel Mercer papers,
   Schomburg Center for Research in Black Culture.
5. South Carolina Educational Radio Network for National Public
   Radio, "Eileen Farrell's American Popular Singers," No. 5
   (New York, November 1, 1981). Tape courtesy of Bart
   Howard.
6. Arnold Shaw, *Fifty Second Street: The Street of Jazz* (New York:
   Quality Paperbacks, 1977), p. 177.
7. Ibid.
8. Bricktop, with Jim Haskins, *Bricktop* (New York: Atheneum
   Publishers, 1983), pp. 237–38.
9. Ibid., p. 246.
10. Whitney Balliett, "Profiles: A Queenly Aura," *The New Yorker*,
    November 18, 1972, p. 62.
11. William Livingstone, "Mabel Mercer: William Livingstone
    Visits With the Singer's Singer," *Stereo Review*, February 1975,
    p. 64.

Chapter V: Her Fifties

1. Art Ford, "Most Un-Appreciated Genius of Popular Music,"
   n.s., n.p. Mabel Mercer papers, Schomburg Center for
   Research in Black Culture.
2. Roland Wild, "She Never Looked Back," *Park East*, March
   1953, p. 16.
3. Ibid., p. 21.

4. Whitney Balliett, "Our Footloose Correspondents: In the Country," *The New Yorker*, September 6, 1982, pp. 42–43.
5. Wild, p. 21.
6. "Mabel Mercer's Life Is Over, But Her Melodies Linger On," *The Chatham Courier*, April 26, 1984, p. 3. Will Craik collection.
7. Ibid.
8. Balliett, p. 43.
9. Dave Garroway, letter to "Annie," May 11, 1954. Mabel Mercer papers, Schomburg Center for Research in Black Culture.
10. Liner notes, "Midnight at Mabel Mercer's," Atlantic Records.
11. Press release, n.d. Mabel Mercer papers, Schomburg.
12. Author's collection.
13. Author's collection.
14. Letter to Jim Haskins from Samuel V. K. Willson, April 3, 1986.
15. "Singer in the Night," *Newsweek*, August 22, 1955, p. 86.
16. Walter Winchell, "Of New York," *The New York Mirror*, September 16, 1955, n.p. Mabel Mercer papers, Schomburg.
17. Letter to Jim Haskins from Walter Ritchie, April 20, 1986.
18. Leonard Lyons, "Lyons Den," *The New York Post*, November 11, 1955, n.p. Mabel Mercer papers, Schomburg.
19. Shirley Fleming, "Mabel Mercer: A Legend in Popular Music," *Hi-Fi Music At Home*, March 1959, p. 23.
20. "Mabel Mercer's OK Recital in G'wich Village at $4.60," *Variety*, October 8, 1958, n.p. Mabel Mercer papers, Schomburg.
21. "Mabel Mercer Sings," *WPAT Gaslight Revue*, August 1964, p. 53. Adelaide Wallin-Beach collection.
22. Ibid.
23. Fleming, pp. 64–65.

Chapter VI. Mabel Out of Fashion

1. Tom Topor, "Daily Closeup," *The New York Post*, November 20, 1972, n.p. Author's collection.
2. Letter to Jim Haskins from Phyllis King Day, April 5, 1986.
3. Gene Lees, "The Magic of Mabel Mercer," *Hi Fi/Stereo Review*, September 1964, p. 65.

4. Letter to Jim Haskins from Lawrence Sharpe, March 31, 1986.
5. Rex Reed, liner notes, *Mabel Mercer & Bobby Short at Town Hall* (Atlantic).
6. Kevin Kelly, "Short Mercer Concert Historic Soul-Touching," *The Boston Globe*, May 23, 1968, n.p.
7. John S. Wilson, "Singers Show Youth Isn't Everything," *The New York Times*, January 21, 1969, n.p.
8. "Mabel Mercer, Bobby Short (Town Hall, N.Y.)," *Variety*, May 28, 1969, p. 26.
9. Letter to Jim Haskins from Peter B. Spivak, April 3, 1986.

Chapter VII. Mabel Back in Fashion

1. Bricktop, with Jim Haskins, *Bricktop* (New York: Atheneum Publishers, 1983), p. 285.
2. Whitney Balliett, "Our Footloose Correspondents: In the Country," *The New Yorker*, September 6, 1982, p. 57.
3. Ibid., pp. 58–60.
4. Rex Reed, ". . . And the Great Mabel Mercer Still Sings at 75," n.s., n.d. Bricktop papers, Schomburg Center for Research in Black Culture.
5. Robert Cushman, "Mabel's Back in Town," *London Observer*, July 10, 1977, p. 28.
6. Frank C. Taylor with Gerald Cook, "Alberta Hunter: The Forgotten Years," *Ms* Magazine, March 1987, pp. 46+.
7. Marian Zalian, "An Ageless Enchantress and Her Timeless Songs," *San Francisco Examiner & Chronicle*, January 29, 1978, p. 17.
8. Letter to Jim Haskins from Samuel V. K. Willson, April 3, 1986.
9. Zalian, p. 17.
10. *Eileen Farrell's American Popular Singers*, National Public Radio series. Tape provided by Bart Howard.

Chapter VIII. Mabel's Last Years

1. Wendell Echols, "Audiophile File," *CRC Newsletter*, August 16, 1980, n.p.
2. Rex Reed, "Great Night for 'Greatest Music Teacher,' " n.s., n.d. Author's collection.

INDEX

James Haskins has written more than sixty nonfiction adult and young adult books, including *Bricktop*, *The Cotton Club*, *Lena Horne*, and *Black Theater in America*. He is professor of English at the University of Florida and lives in New York City.